The Holy Spirit

by

Barbara Ann Payne

The Holy Spirit

© 2018 Barbara Ann Payne

All Scripture quotations are taken from the New King James Version of the Bible unless otherwise stated.

Published by Select Arrow, the publishing arm of United in Christ
www.unitedinchrist.co.uk

ISBN: 1986145816

Cover design and interior layout: Homer Slack
Editor: Angela Slack
Proof Reader: Lynda Smith

Printed by CreateSpace

ACKNOWLEDGEMENTS

I want to thank my dear friends Homer and Angela Slack who have encouraged and supported me in writing and publishing this book.

My prayer partner Chris who has diligently prayed for me and urged me to write this book.

My husband John who has kept cups of tea flowing into the office and his support during this labour of love.

Most of all You Jesus without whom I would not know the precious Holy Spirit.

Table of Contents

Preface

The primary reason for writing this book is for new Christians to gain some insight as to who the Holy Spirit is. If you are truly born again, you will have already experienced His power through your salvation but it does not end there; there is so much more.

When I became born again, it was in the power of the Holy Spirit with true conviction, repentance and tears of joy. A supernatural happening that took place within me. I attended many gatherings where the manifestation of the Holy Spirit resulted in salvation, healing and deliverance[1] for many people. I believe one of the reasons we are not experiencing growth in the Church today is because the Holy Spirit is not being allowed to lead and manifest His presence through the gifts. There is also a lack of teaching about who He is and the exciting life we can have when we allow Him to lead us. *"Those who are led by the Spirit are the Sons of God".* Romans 8:14

Men are trying to build their own churches today and the Holy Spirit sometimes gets a mention but I have interviewed many Christians who do not really understand who He is and why we need Him and they have encouraged me to write this book.

Over my 40 years of being a believer, I have come to know Him in a deeper way and my heart's desire is that we give Jesus His Church back and allow the Holy Spirit to function within it. Then and only then will we see the Church grow, otherwise known as revival.

"He that hath an ear let him hear what the spirit saith to the churches."
Revelation Chapters 2-3

---

[1] Released from demonic strongholds or the bondage that results from substance abuse etc.

Chapter 1

Who Is He?

Much has been written down in the Scriptures and in Timothy 3:16 Paul states: *"All Scripture is God breathed and profitable for doctrine, reproof, for correction and training in righteousness."* That being the case, what can we learn about the Holy Spirit from Scripture? There is so much to know about Him and know Him we must if we are to serve Jesus Christ.

"For as many as are led by the Spirit of God, these are sons of God." Romans 8:14.

We are exhorted to follow after the Spirit and not the flesh so we need to know who we are following; we cannot follow someone we do not know. So as we are led by the Spirit we need to know who He really is.

There really is no mystery about the Holy Spirit, He was there at the beginning of time and He is there at the end and before we get to the end of this book you will be able to see who He is and how He is manifested throughout Scripture. His foretelling, His abiding and role in our lives.

Genesis 1:2 states, *"The earth was without form and void, and darkness*

1

was on the face of the deep. And the Spirit of God was hovering over the face of the waters." Verse 26 says: *"Let us make man in our image."* Also, Revelation 22:17 states, *"And the Spirit and the Bride say, come."*

He has been from the beginning of time. He was there when man was made so He knows just as much about us as God the Father and Jesus. He will be until the end of time as we know it.

*****

I would like to share with you my own thoughts on who He is and I have used simple illustrations which I hope will help. I found this an easy way of explaining the Trinity known as the Godhead. *"For in Him dwells all the fullness of the Godhead bodily."* Colossians 2:9

He is the third person of the Holy Trinity – Trinity meaning three. Genesis 1:26 says: *"let us make man in our image..."* and we naturally ask ourselves how many is the us? In God's Word we are told that there are three and we tend to call it the Trinity whereas I prefer to call it the Godhead as also in Romans 1:20 it states, *"For since the creation of the world His invisible attributes are clearly seen, being understood by the things that are made, even His eternal power and Godhead, so that they are without excuse."*

The Holy Spirit's Place In The Godhead

God The Father: Commander/Visionary/Creator
First operationally.
In Genesis chapter 1 the very first line says, *"In the beginning God..."* and goes on to say things like, *"Let there be, Let us make man..."* and *"be fruitful..."* He states what has to be done, He commands.

2

Jesus Christ: The Doer

Not second in priority but second operationally.

You can find many Scriptures where Jesus says, *"For I do not speak of my own accord, but the Father who sent me commanded me what to say and how to say it. I know that His command leads to eternal life. So whatever I say is just what the Father has told me to say."* John chapter 12: 49-50, There are other Scriptures you can find in John 14: 10, 24, 31. where Jesus does the will of His Father.

Holy Spirit: The Empowerer

Not third in priority but third operationally

Luke 4:14 says; *"Jesus returned after 40 days in the desert in the power of the Spirit."* Note that He was led into the desert by the Holy Spirit but came out in power. He passed the test of love obedience and commitment to the Father. There is no power without being tested and as we continue to read through this book you will read of many times God gives instructions that must be obeyed. When we obey, the Holy Spirit comes or works through us in power.

In Acts 1:8 we read *"You shall receive power after the Holy Ghost (Spirit) has come."* I don't know what you imagine the word power to mean but it certainly does not mean to 'zap' like in comic book illustrations, it's not that kind of power. Yes it is demonstrated in many forms but this also means to give legal authority to or to authorise. An example of that could be when someone is given power of attorney over someone's affairs. It is legal authority to act on behalf of another person.

God the Father, God the Son and God the Holy Spirit are all co-workers together, interdependent, never in disunity or contradiction, always in perfect harmony. But God's Word always has the final say.

Another example the Holy Spirit gave me was with a light switch:

Light switch: this tells the light to go on.

Bulb: this immediately turns the bulb to light.

Wiring: this is the unseen power that connects the switch and the bulb, you cannot see it but you know it is there.

Every time you switch on that light it is by faith that you expect the light will come on. Not one will work without the other. The switch can be on the wall looking good, the bulb in the fitting ready to be lit up but if there's no wiring plugged into the power supply to connect everything there will never be any power so there will be no light.

I know some Christians are like this, they look good, know lots of Scripture and want to serve God but there is no power in their lives.

There is one man (apart from Jesus) who I think actually experienced the Godhead Acts 7:55 tells us about Stephen. "*But he, being full of the Holy Ghost, looked up steadfastly into heaven, and saw the glory of God, and Jesus standing on the right hand of God and said: 'Behold, I see the heavens opened, and the Son of man standing on the right hand of God.'*" (KJV) He was Full of the Holy Spirit and saw Jesus standing at the right hand side of God. All this whilst he was being stoned for his faith, it makes me wonder what Stephen would have become had he not been martyred. Maybe his martyrdom was for the best as it teaches us about faith and trust in God.

His Personage

We are going to see how the Holy Spirit is a person with characteristics and not a 'ghostly' apparition or force but a person and a gentleman too. During my time as a Christian I have heard and seen many things done 'in the spirit' and I wonder what spirit they were done in. As I sought to learn about Him I found out some wonderful truths, as well as making some mistakes too. I was always looking to mature

4

Christians for answers and most of the time they gave them to me but the more I read God's Word the more I began to realise that the Holy Spirit is a person. Not a ghostly apparition or something that turns up when we shout the loudest or even worse, when we try to manipulate Him into doing something so that we can say we 'moved in the spirit'[2], God help us.

Some believe you can have a bit of Him? There is only one Holy Spirit and He is a person and you cannot have a 'bit of HIM'. You either have HIM or you do not. This is why we need to get to know Him as a person, someone who is with us constantly as we seek to serve God.

He Speaks:
"Therefore as the Holy Spirit says..." Hebrews 3:7, *"However when He, the Spirit of Truth has come He will guide you into all truth, for He will not speak on His own authority, but whatever He hears He speaks."* John 16:13, *"And the Spirit and the bride say, 'Come'!"* Revelation 22:17, *"Then the Spirit said to Philip..."* Acts 8:29, *"As they ministered to the Lord and fasted the Holy Spirit said..."* Acts 13:2, *"Then the Spirit told me to go with them, doubting nothing. Moreover these six brethren accompanied me, and we entered the man's house."* Acts 11:12 These Scriptures reveal the fact that the Holy Spirit speaks.

He Hears:
The story of Ananias & Sapphira lying to the Holy Spirit that led to their deaths. Acts 5.

He Leads:
"Jesus was led by the Spirit into the wilderness." Luke 4:1. As many as are led by the Spirit they are the sons of God. Romans 8:14.

---

[2] To experience or accomplish something by the working of God's Spirit

The Holy Spirit also...

- Hides and protects: Psalm 119:114
- Comforts: John 16:7, John: 15:26
- Directs: Acts 16:6-7
- Manifests Himself: 1 Corinthians chapter 12
- Brings unity and power: Acts 4:31-32
- Prays: Romans 8:26
- Sanctifies: Romans 15:16
- Teaches: 1 John 2:27, Luke 12:12, John 14:26
- He is The Wonderful Counsellor: John 14:25
- Helps: John 14:16, John 14:26
- Guides: Romans 8:14, 1 John 2:27
- He is The Spirit of Truth: John 14:17
- Witnesses: Acts 5:32, 20:23

Let us not forget also, that Jesus was conceived by the Holy Spirit. "*And the angel answered and said to her; 'The Holy Spirit will come upon you and the power of the Highest will overshadow you; therefore, also, that Holy One who is to be born will be called the Son of God.'*" Luke 1:35

These characteristics speak of a person who can teach, hear, speak, guide, lead, pray and write. You may not have thought about these things before but when Jesus said, "*I will not leave you as orphans but will send you a Helper,*" understand that, the helper had to be someone very real and very special. I pray that so far you can see how precious the gift of the Holy Spirit is to us. I have experienced the power of the Holy Spirit myself in my own body, He has healed me of epilepsy and smoking. He healed me from Angina as well as from the emotional and physical effects of sexual abuse as a child. I have written a short account of these in my book 'Reach for your Miracle.' So I do not write out of study alone but also out of experience of the power of the Holy Spirit in my life. This is the sole reason for writing this book to share testimonies and to confirm through God's Word that The Holy Spirit is a Person and a gentleman who will not force His way into our lives.

Names Given Him Throughout Scripture

As a new Christian reading the Bible was not easy and there were so many things I did not understand and still don't. I believe that is quite normal and this is where you need a mature spiritual teacher to help you. I was very blessed to have a pastor who was also a teacher and evangelist. Who had been taught by the Holy Spirit. He was very patient with me as I had so many questions about the Holy Spirit. I am sure I got on his nerves; nevertheless he did have the patience of a saint. He always had the time and above all the desire to share the Word of God.

There was no internet as such then or celebrity speakers and not many books. I think personally that it was great and I thank God for my pastor Jim Sweet and his wife Joyce for some of the most memorable Spirit filled Bible studies I have ever received. One of the questions I asked him was about who the Holy Spirit was and the difference between Him and the Holy Ghost?

He began to show me that the Holy Spirit can be seen under many names in Scripture and that opened up a whole new avenue for me when reading. I began understanding more what I was reading and I would like to share them with you now.

One word can mean many things such as the original Hebrew word for Spirit which means air, anger, blast, breath, cool courage, mind, spirit, wind, windy and make of quick understanding. It is also spelt the same in Arabic and means wind, mind and spirit.

Therefore we see that the Holy Spirit is often referred to by different names but His different characteristics can be understood from the meaning of these names and the different forms He takes. We will look at these in the next chapter.

In the Scriptures, some of the last words that Jesus spoke can be found in the last book of the Bible - Revelation, *"he that hath an ear let him hear what the Spirit says unto the Church."* As the Church of Jesus Christ He has commanded us to listen to what the Holy Spirit is saying to us. The Holy Spirit is here to help us, lead us, guide us, strengthen us and empower us to build the Kingdom of God.

Chapter 2

Attributes of the Holy Spirit

We have looked at the person of the Holy Spirit and His part within the Godhead, now let us take a look at some of His attributes.

He is like Oil

He is often represented in Scripture as oil, and oil does a specific job when it is added to an engine of a car/lorry etc. It cleanses and stops the engine from seizing up. Driving an engine without oil will cause friction, overheating and it will eventually seize up. Oil has a soothing, restorative effect too and it is used in many aromatherapy treatments to treat the skin. Oil is also a fuel that is needed for light, energy or power. From these analogies you can fully appreciate how multifunctional and multidimensional the role of the Holy Spirit in our life is.

In the Old Testament, oil was used by appointed prophets to anoint those given Godly authority. In 1 Samuel chapters 15 and 16, we see Samuel a prophet of God (you can read about how he came to be a prophet in the first chapter), who had God given authority to anoint future kings and give them direction through prophecy.

In this chapter of the Bible we find that because of Saul's disobedience to God, the kingdom was torn from him and God required Samuel to anoint a future king which in this case was David. Samuel would carry a horn filled with oil. As Samuel was brought up in the Temple where many oils were used I would imagine that his horn would be filled with frankincense, myrrh and maybe other fragrant oils. This prophetic office gave them the authority to carry out the function that God was calling them to fulfil.

In Matthew 25:1, Jesus speaks of the wise and foolish virgins and the wise virgins made sure they had oil in their lamps so they were not found wanting when the Bridegroom comes. We as Christians need to ensure that we are filled with 'The Oil' (the Holy Spirit) so we are not found wandering in the dark when Jesus returns but have the light of the Holy Spirit burning bright within us to be ready to meet Him. This is a teaching all on its own and it is well worth reading this whole chapter through.

He is like Fire

One of the purposes of fire is to burn rubbish. If rubbish is not burned up it smells and causes infestation and all kinds of bacteria, germs and disease. Fire has a purifying effect and eliminates those smells caused by rubbish.

We need to be cleansed from the sin in our lives and this is the attribute of The Holy Spirit that will cleanse us from all the dirt that sin has produced. *"...and there appeared before them cloven tongues like as a fire, and it sat upon each of them."*Acts 2:3. John the baptist states; *"I indeed baptise you with water unto repentance, but He who comes after me is mightier than I, whose shoes I am not worthy to bear: He shall baptise you with the Holy Ghost and with Fire."* Matthew 3:11

He is like Wind

Wind is an unseen power. You don't know where it has come from or where it will end up, but you know where it has been by the evidence it leaves in its wake. You only have to watch the evidence in our newscasts to see devastation caused by a tsunami or typhoon, they have amazing power. But it can also be a very gentle breeze that soothes and cools you from the heat.

"...and suddenly there came a sound from heaven as of a rushing mighty wind, and it filled the entire house where they were sitting." Acts 2:2 *"The wind blows where it wishes, and you hear the sound of it, but cannot tell where it comes from and where it goes. So is everyone who is born of the Spirit."* John 3:8

He is like a Dove

This is probably the one attribute that we are more familiar with as it is often used as a Christian emblem on jewellery brooches, literature and is often used in graphics to represent peace. The dove depicts peace and tranquillity and when you see a dove it is pure white and can make you feel peaceful and gentle.

"...and the Holy Ghost descended in a bodily shape like a dove upon Him, and a voice came from heaven saying: 'Thou art my beloved son in whom I am well pleased." Luke 3:22 Also in Matthew 3:16, *"When He had been baptized, Jesus came up immediately from the water; and behold, the heavens were opened to Him, and He saw the Spirit of God descending like a dove and alighting upon Him."*

"And John bore witness, saying, 'I saw the Spirit descending from heaven like a dove, and He remained upon Him. I did not know Him, but He who sent me to baptize with water said to me, Upon whom you see the Spirit descending, and remaining on Him, this is He who baptizes with

the Holy Spirit. And I have seen and testified that this is the Son of God." John 1:32-34

"...for the kingdom of God is not eating and drinking, but righteousness and peace and joy in the Holy Spirit." Romans 14:17

It is a worthy note here that after Jesus was baptised in the Holy Spirit that the Holy Spirit led Him into the wilderness. I have mentioned twice before that the sons of God are led by the Spirit and here we see that even Jesus was led by the Holy Spirit after being baptised.

He is like Water

Water's chemical formula is made up of 3 elements, H_2O. Each water molecule is made of two hydrogen atoms and one oxygen atom, thus there are two "H" atoms and one "O". The atoms are joined by covalent bonding, meaning that they share electrons (as opposed to ionic bonding, in which atoms completely transfer electrons) What is interesting is that even the formula reflects harmony of purpose, the 3 atoms share the power of the electrons.

Further reading:

You can find out much more about water and its composition if you are interested at http://www.all-water.org/Chemistry.html.

We see water in everyday life as steam/vapour/gas that rises up or floats around or liquid that runs along surfaces with great power or placid calm, or as solid blocks of unmovable ice. It is refreshing, cleansing and we become ill or can even die of dehydration without it. We appreciate the necessity of water especially when we are thirsty. Jesus says, *"But whoever drinks of the water that I shall give him shall never thirst; but the water that I shall give him shall be in him a well of water springing up into everlasting life."* John 4:14

"On the last day, that great day of the feast, Jesus stood and cried out, saying, 'If anyone thirsts, let him come to Me and drink. He who believes in Me, as the Scripture has said, out of his heart will flow rivers of living water.' But this He spoke concerning the Spirit, whom those believing in Him would receive;" John 7:37-39

He is the Breath of God

"And when He [Jesus] had said this, He breathed on them, and said unto them, 'Receive ye the Holy Ghost.'" John 20:22

"Now may the God of hope fill you with all joy and peace in believing, that you may abound in hope by the power of the Holy Spirit." Romans 15:13

As I mentioned before, the Holy Spirit will not force His way into our lives or make us do anything, especially things that oppose the Word of God. He is a gentleman, a person of many characteristics and attributes and Jesus sent Him so we would not be left as orphans after His ascension. He is the third person of the Trinity. He is the Author of the Word of God and He will never do anything contrary to it, only to confirm it.

He sent Him to be:
- Comforter
- Friend
- Teacher
- Guide
- Empowerer
- Helper

I have witnessed some irreverent behaviour accredited to the Holy Spirit and this has turned people away from God altogether. Examples are grunting like pigs, mooing like cows, growling like dogs, just to name a few. A friend of mine would not listen to anything said about the Holy Spirit because of this sort of behaviour in a large gathering, she was so afraid she would be made to do this and not have any control. May God forgive us for allowing this to happen in the assembly of Christians who meet in the name of Jesus.

I repeat the Holy Spirit is a gentleman who gently leads us into all truth, sanctifies us and above all leads us to Jesus.

Chapter 3

Promise and Outpouring

We have mentioned that the Holy Spirit has been around from the beginning of creation and will be with us until Jesus comes in the book of Revelation. His outpouring is now available for all who will receive Jesus as their Saviour.

The Promise

Before we look at this amazing historical event we need to go back into the Old Testament to read its foretelling. *"In the last days I will pour out My Spirit on All Flesh. Your sons and your daughters will prophesy. Your old men will dream dreams. Your young men shall see visions and also on My maidservants and on My menservants I will pour out My Spirit in those days."* Joel 2:27 This was a prophetic word from Joel, one of the Minor prophets in the Old Testament and was written approximately 800 years before Jesus Christ came.

When I was taught to read the Bible I was given some wonderful advice that I have always used these past 40 years and it has helped me to avoid reading the Scripture out of context and it was this: When reading any verse in the Bible ask yourself:

- Who is speaking?
- Who is speaking to whom?
- What is the cultural background?

So with this in mind let us take a further look at this passage of Scripture. It was the prophet Joel who was speaking. He was a prophet of Israel and was speaking to the Nation of Israel and its Elders. He is speaking of an event that must take place in the future of Israel as a nation, after much desolation and wickedness. He was calling for them to repent and foretelling things that must take place in the future. The Holy Spirit was upon him, allowing him to see into the future. In the book of Ezekiel chapter 11:19 It states, *"Then I will give them one heart, and I will put a new Spirit within them and take the stony heart out of their flesh and give them a heart of flesh."* There are not many more prophecies like Joel's as it is very specific but there are many Scriptures that imply this event, one is Isaiah 44:3 *"For I will pour water on him who is thirsty, and floods on the dry ground; I will pour My Spirit on your descendants, and My blessing on your offspring."*

In John's gospel from chapters 14 to 16 Jesus talks about the Holy Spirit's coming. He said that He must go so that the Holy Spirit can come, He calls the Holy Spirit the Helper. Jesus Himself promised that He will send Him to us. John's gospel is one of my favourite books because as a new Christian it was in this gospel that the Holy Spirit revealed Himself to me personally. There is nothing quite like receiving a revelation for yourself when reading God's Word.

Jesus' words are the most powerful and as we read in the Acts of the apostles chapter 1, we can read these wonderful words that He spoke. Let us remember these are the words of the resurrected Christ. *"And He (Jesus) being assembled together with them, He commanded them not to depart from Jerusalem but to wait for the promise of the Father which, He said, 'you have heard from Me; for John truly baptised with water, but you shall be baptised with the Holy Spirit not many days from now."* Acts 1: 4-5

And again *"...but you shall receive power when the Holy Spirit has come upon you; and you shall be my witnesses unto Me in Jerusalem and in all Judea and Samaria, and unto the ends of the earth."* Verse 8

John gave this testimony in his gospel chapter 1: 33-34: *"The man on whom you see the Spirit descend and remain is the one who will baptise with the Holy Spirit. I have seen and do testify that this is God's chosen one."* (NIV)

So when did this actually happen?

The Outpouring

The promise of His coming was fulfilled shortly after Jesus' death, resurrection and ascension. It was fulfilled in a very specific and timely way. It all took place on the day of Pentecost as recorded in Acts chapter 2.

Jesus never said or did anything unless His Father told Him to or showed Him and He particularly told the disciples to *"Wait in Jerusalem."* Jesus specifically said: *"...not many days from now."*

I wondered about this and so began to ask the Holy Spirit to show me. As I said earlier we have to look at Scripture in context and so looking at the culture we can see that a) Jesus was Jewish b) He celebrated all the feasts that were ordained by God (not men) and above all His mission on earth was to *"fulfil the Law and the prophets"* Matthew 5:17

17

So here we see the disciples in Jerusalem during the Feast of Weeks (the counting of the Omer,[3] occurs over a period of 7 weeks or 49 days) The 50th day was the day of Pentecost and 50 in the Hebrew means freedom. This was the very day when the Holy Spirit was given. It is also believed by some that this same festival was when the law was given to Moses on Mount Sinai. Now we can begin to understand why this particular date was chosen by God and why Jesus told them to 'wait'. The amazing outpouring happened in the Holy city of Jerusalem at the right time and in the right place.

The disciples were the first to receive power and this is culminated in their freedom from sin and fear. From henceforth they would go and preach the gospel of the Kingdom of God. This amazing gospel, that brings the law of God into our hearts, through the regeneration of our spirit by the Holy Spirit. That's when you know in your knower that you have been born again, John chapter 3.

When the outpouring of God's Holy Spirit happened it was not a quiet affair. People could see flames of fire; they could hear the rushing of a mighty wind something quite unusual was happening that must have brought fear too. Even though this was happening there were many in the crowds that still mocked what was going on so, Peter stood up to explain saying, *"...this is the prophetic word given by Joel."* Acts 2:16

Weakness turned to power:
In Acts 3, after the outpouring of the Holy Spirit, Peter and John were on their way to the temple when they healed a man at the Gate called Beautiful. They were amazed at what was being accomplished through this new found faith and boldness/obedience. They had no idea on that day what would happen, they just let the Holy Spirit lead them.

---

[3]This is a celebration of the First Fruits of harvest. During this period of 49 days the disciples would have been reciting the daily prayer of blessing.

Even though they were seized and thrown into prison they still continued to preach about Jesus. Peter stood up in the Sanhedrin (this was an assembly of between twenty three and seventy one various bodies that made up the Jewish Judicial system) and preached repentance to the leaders. When they saw the boldness and courage of these men they took note that they had been with Jesus. This caused the Sanhedrin to be afraid because the truth was standing right in front of them, the man that was once a cripple was now completely well. So, they let them off with a warning not to speak any more about this Jesus. Peter went on to discover the blessings of this newly given Holy Spirit outpouring. He was now able to discern Spirits[4] and even later had a Word of Knowledge[5] about Ananias and Sapphira.

Power in the Church
The coming of the Holy Spirit also signifies the birth of the Church. No doubt the Church was destined to be born in power. In this context we read about Ananias and Sapphira telling Peter a lie but if you take a closer look we see that Peter said they lied to the Holy Spirit. This kind of boldness showed a very different Peter. Peter is a new man and the difference came after he received the baptism in the Holy Spirit. Peter is now being led by the Spirit and not by the flesh/fear. A wonderful transformation from the Peter who was afraid of being recognized as a follower of Jesus at the night of Jesus' arrest, to this man who now stood before religious leaders unafraid of any consequences. As we read more of Peter's life we are able to witness God working through him by the power of the Holy Spirit.

I am sure there are many other accounts that were not recorded. One of my favourite characters in the book of Acts is Stephen. We read of how the power of the Holy Spirit enabled him to die with words

---

[4] Able to tell the difference between God's Holy Spirit and other spirits.
[5] A word given by God about a situation or person that no one else knows about.

of forgiveness on his lips, just as Jesus did. He prayed, *"Father forgive them for they know not what they do."* Acts 8: 60

Today we are privileged to have so much evidence and examples of the move of God on and after the day of Pentecost. It must have been amazing to have been there to be part of this fulfilment of prophecy and to experience the amazing power of God. We should remember here that the disciples would have had no idea of what and how the Holy Spirit would look or be like and how it would affect them. They were willing to trust that Jesus, even though He had gone to the Father, would keep His promise to them. What a promise!

That promise is still for us today. There is no account in Scripture where the Holy Spirit went back to heaven because from that day forward it was the beginning of the Church. The real Church, born of the Holy Spirit and down through the last 2000 years has seen many accounts of saints having the same baptism in the same Holy Spirit and demonstrating the same power.

Chapter 4

His Indwelling

Whether you are a Bible student or not it would be good at this time, just to read the gospel of John chapters 14, 15 and 16. Here you will see Jesus affirming and reaffirming the fact that the Holy Spirit will live in the believer. Listen to what He said in John 14:15-18 *"If you love Me keep my commandments and I will pray to the Father and He will give you another Comforter, that He may abide with you forever, even the Spirit of Truth. The world cannot accept Him because it neither sees Him nor knows Him. But you know Him for He lives with you and will be in you."* Yes, He now dwells within the believer.

We know where He comes from. Jesus sent Him after He ascended into Heaven. In John 16:7, Jesus goes on to say that He will not leave us as orphans and this precious Holy Spirit has been sent to us to help us to live the life Jesus would have us live. To comfort us in times of trouble, to manifest His power when we are serving in the Kingdom, so that God can be glorified in everything we do. The Holy Spirit is real and for 'born again' believers, is a reality that sometimes can be difficult to explain to others and often misunderstood but He can be demonstrated. We have now come to the reality of God's Word that the Holy Spirit dwells in a born again believer's life. It amazes me that this has happened throughout generations and will continue to happen

21

until Jesus returns.

When we read of the Holy Spirit in the Old Testament there does not appear to be a dwelling place for Him but there are times when He worked through chosen people. This was usually to fulfil certain tasks or for prophesying. Some examples of these can be found in Exodus 31:1-11, *"Then the Lord said, 'See I have chosen Bezalel son of Uri the son of Hur, of the tribe of Judah, and have filled him with the Spirit of God, with wisdom and understanding, with knowledge and all kinds of skills – to make artistic designs for work in gold, silver and bronze, to cut and set stones, to work in wood and to engage in all kinds of crafts.'"*

This is wonderful to read because the Israelites had been in bondage over 400 years and therefore the only skill they knew was building bricks for Pharaoh's pyramids and palaces. The work now was to build the Tabernacle as a dwelling place for God. I assume they had no idea what to do so God filled them full of His Spirit, inspired them and showed them how to work with various resources. He actually showed them the pattern of the Tabernacle that is in heaven for them to work from. See Hebrews chapters 8 and 9.

Another example is in Numbers 11:26 where Eldad and Medad were given special abilities by the Spirit of God. In 1 Samuel 16:13 we see the Spirit moving on David. It says, *"...and from that day on the Spirit of the Lord came powerfully upon David..."* and, of course, we also see Him coming upon many of the prophets in the Old Testament. Look at Elijah in 1st and 2nd Kings and how Elisha asked for a double portion of God's Spirit. All these make exciting reading and give us a deeper understanding of how the Spirit of God worked in an Old Testament context.

As you continue to read the Old Testament you will see clearly that the Holy Spirit came upon some people. After the Day of Pentecost however, the Holy Spirit not only now comes upon us but also dwells within the believer.

Jesus makes this statement in John's Gospel, *"It is to your advantage that I go away, for if I do not go away the Helper* [Holy Spirit] *will not come to you: but if I depart I will send Him to you."* Jesus never says anything that is not true because He is The Truth.

Today He dwells within the hearts of His people who are born again and have received the baptism in the Holy Spirit. *"He who raised Christ Jesus from the dead will also give life to your mortal bodies through His Spirit who dwells in you."* Romans 8:11. Jesus also said,: *"And I will pray the Father, and He will give you another Helper, that He may abide with you forever."* John 14:16 The word abide means to remain, endure, continue and tarry forever.

So in the Old Testament the Spirit of God came and went but in the New Testament He abides within His people. What a Mighty God we serve His ways are past finding out.

*****

"Or do you not know that your body is the temple of the Holy Spirit who is in you, whom you have from God, and you are not your own? For you were bought at a price; therefore glorify God in your body and in your spirit, which are God's." 1 Corinthians 6:19

Chapter 5

His Role and Function

These are the words of Jesus in, John 16:13-16 *"However, when He, the Spirit of truth, has come, He will guide you into all truth; for He will not speak on His own authority, but whatever He hears He will speak; and He will tell you things to come. He will glorify Me, for He will take of what is Mine and declare it to you. All things that the Father has are Mine. Therefore I said that He will take of Mine and declare it to you."*

I used to occasionally go to an Assemblies of God Church in Wigan, Lancashire, that held special conferences throughout the year and they were fantastic. One day I noticed that on the wall above the platform were written these words.

"It's not by might nor by power but by my spirit says the Lord." Zechariah 4:6

I did not understand the full meaning then, it was just a lovely Scripture to me but over the years I have studied and learned who His Spirit is. I have however, witnessed many efforts in man's strength that should have been left to the power of the Holy Spirit. I have also witnessed the power of the Holy Spirit in my own life and in the lives of others and there is a very distinctive difference between a life in the Holy Spirit and a life lived in the flesh.

Jesus told His disciples to wait in Jerusalem until they be endued with power from on high; It is only after this momentous event in history that the Disciples of Christ began their ministry with boldness demonstrated with the manifestation of the Holy Spirit. We have numerous accounts of such events in the book of the Acts of the apostles.

The outpouring of the Holy Spirit was all new to the disciples. In their early years Jesus was there with them to practically demonstrate the Power of God. After this amazing outpouring, they now had to exercise their own faith in what Jesus had promised. Peter was the first to exercise this new found faith and boldness.

Fear turned to boldness:
Peter lied about his association with Jesus and before Jesus was crucified had denied Him three times but after he received the Holy Spirit, he boldly went on to tell the crowd they must be saved by repenting and being baptized and they will receive the Holy Spirit. In fact he publicly accused the crowd of crucifying Jesus! People who were cut to their hearts quickly repented and were baptized. Over 3,000 souls were added to the Church that day. That once fearful man was now filled with boldness, not just for a moment or for a day but until the end of his life.

Here we see the first function in the Spirit was to witness of who Jesus is and the result was that many were saved that day.

Why do we need the Holy Spirit?
We need Him to witness of Jesus, *"But you shall receive power when*

the Holy Spirit has come upon you; and you shall be witnesses to Me in Jerusalem, and in all Judea and Samaria, and to the end of the earth." Acts 1:8

We need Him to interpret God's Word to our hearts, after all, He wrote it through men of faith. If you try reading Scripture without Him it will just be a dead letter and a history book but when you have Him within the Word of God comes alive. It is like living water that runs over the soul and makes us hunger for more of Jesus.

"Beloved, now we are children of God; and it has not yet been revealed what we shall be, but we know that when He is revealed, we shall be like Him, for we shall see Him as He is." 1 John 3:3 This is a mystery that none can fathom except to know that God's Word is a Living Word and it changes you from the inside. I know this from personal experience and you can read some of this in my book 'Reach for your Miracle' or in the SHARE Magazine. https://issuu.com/thesharemagazine/docs/vol2-iss2/8

In 1 John chapter 5 we read, *"It is the Holy Spirit that bears witness to the Truth because the Spirit is Truth."* The Holy Spirit draws us to Jesus and Jesus reveals the Father to us. His function is to lead people to Jesus to convict men, women boys and girls of sin and to show them the Saviour who can forgive and wash away all their sins.

His work is to sanctify us that we become more like Jesus and sons of God so that we no longer conform to worldly things but set our hearts on heavenly things. *"But we are bound to give thanks to God always for you, brethren beloved by the Lord, because God from the beginning chose you for salvation through sanctification by the Spirit and belief in the truth."* 2 Thess. 2:13

He has been given to us for the works of God here on earth, within His Kingdom. We cannot accomplish any work without Him. Oh, we can do good works and practical things but when God manifests Himself by the power of His Spirit through His disciples it is very powerful and above all, brings glory to God.

This is why He sent Him, to empower us to preach the FULL gospel, of His death and resurrection. To lay hands on the sick or blind etc. and to bind up the broken hearted. To release the captives that are bound, bringing great glory and testimony to God.

Mark 16.14-18 says, *"Later He appeared to the eleven as they sat at the table; and He rebuked their unbelief and hardness of heart, because they did not believe those who had seen Him after He had risen. And He said to them, 'Go into all the world and preach the gospel to every creature. He who believes and is baptized will be saved; but he who does not believe will be condemned. And these signs will follow those who believe: In My name they will cast out demons; they will speak with new tongues; they will take up serpents; and if they drink anything deadly, it will by no means hurt them; they will lay hands on the sick, and they will recover'."*

This is all by the power of the Holy Spirit working signs and wonders through us as we preach the gospel. We need Him to overcome the world because although we live in this world we are not part of it anymore. Our lives belong to God and His purposes within His Kingdom. The Holy Spirit guides and leads us to be obedient followers of our Lord Jesus, overcoming the temptations of sin. The Holy Spirit helps us to keep our eyes on Jesus.

We need the Holy Spirit to live the Christian life and to serve God in Spirit and in Truth. In Romans 8 the apostle Paul had much to say about walking in the Spirit and not walking after the flesh. We need Him in our prayer life as we cannot enter the realm of Spiritual Warfare or Intercession without Him. *"Likewise the Spirit also helps in our weaknesses. For we do not know what we should pray for as we ought, but the Spirit Himself makes intercession for us with groanings which cannot be uttered."* Romans 8:26-27

In my time, I have been in some amazing Holy Spirit meetings and some meetings where men have tried to whip up something that looks like the Spirit which has had nothing to do with God. Maybe this is why so many churches are closing because the Holy Spirit has been left out of most of them. There seems to be so much fear about what He will do because we want to stay in control of everything and not hand the control over to Him. Acts 5:42 says, *"And every day in the temple and in people's homes they continued to teach and preach the Good News about Jesus."* Threats and sufferings did not prevent them from preaching the Good News and witnessing.

What an amazing change came into the lives of the apostles after Pentecost. Instead of seeking first place they now became servants. Instead of being angry and returning evil for evil they now had love and compassion and a forgiving heart. Instead of running away when things got difficult, they were bold and stood strong and they were even ready to die for their faith if necessary.

This was the power of the Holy Spirit mixed with their faith. How I would long to see those days again, wouldn't you? It is at this point we should remind ourselves that the Holy Spirit was sent so we can boldly proclaim who Jesus is and why He came.

The apostle Paul's ministry followed not long after the Day of Pentecost and during his time in ministry he travelled to many places encouraging the believers and demonstrating the power of God through the work of the Holy Spirit. *"And my speech and my preaching were not with persuasive words of human wisdom, but in demonstration of the Spirit and of power."* 1 Corinthians 2:4

In some Christian denominations/groups they would like to tell you that the Holy Spirit was only for the disciples at that time and that He did not carry on after they died. Well, all I can say is, they have not read all the Scriptures and also how do they think the church is still growing today, even in the face of great persecution? In the book of Ephesians it states that Jesus gave Spiritual gifts to the Church for the building of the Church. Paul exhorts the Church to not quench the Spirit (see 1 Thessalonians 5:19) chapter 4:8 states, *"Therefore he who rejects this does not reject man, but God, who has also given us His Holy Spirit."*

Jesus led His disciples into truth, they did not lead Him and the Holy Spirit is to lead us into all truth, we do not lead Him.

Chapter 6

The Body
of Christ

"For as the body is one, and has many members, and all the members of that one body, being many, are one body; so also is Christ: for by one Spirit we are all baptised into one body, whether we be Jew or Gentile, whether we are slave or free; and have all been made to drink into one Spirit, for the body is not one member but many." 1 Corinthian 12:12-14

Most people use the term church loosely without much idea of what church means. People often think of the many denominations which only adds to the confusion as to what is The Church? One can understand their confusion as there are many churches across the world that has many different titles as well as many different kinds of services. They include Church of England (the recognised state Church in the United Kingdom), Baptist, Methodist, Catholic and evangelical to name but a few. There are also many other religions that give the impression that they are a church but have no resemblance whatsoever to the ONE TRUE CHURCH OF JESUS CHRIST as stated by the apostle Paul in the New Testament Scriptures.

Other religions that try to resemble Christianity but are not, includesthe Church of Jesus Christ Of Latter Day Saints, Jehovah's Witnesses, the

New Age movement and others. *"For if he who comes preaches another Jesus whom we have not preached, or if you receive a different Spirit which you have not received, or a different gospel which you have not accepted—you may well put up with it!"* 2 Corinthians 11:4

As a new Christian I was also confused and so were many Christians I have met. No wonder that unbelievers are confused if we are. There is a difference between Christianity and other religions. In other religions you have to be part of a movement and there is usually a hierarchy with someone who is at the head who founded the movement. True Christianity bears no resemblance to any of these. Unlike these other religions, Christianity was birthed by the Holy Spirit on the day of Pentecost, not by any human. True Christianity is all about having a personal relationship with Jesus Christ. It is personal and intimate.

Once you begin to read and understand what the Church really is and where it began, if you should delve into Church history, you will be able to see the one true Church. The apostle Paul calls it The Body of Christ.

Religion in the dictionary is defined as the belief in and worship of a god or gods, or any such system of belief and worship: e.g. the Christian religion. (When used informally) an activity that someone is extremely enthusiastic about and does regularly: e.g. "Football is a religion for these people." (Cambridge dictionary). Religion therefore is something you practice regularly whether it is with a group of people or not. The definition of Church is quite different.

Having defined religion we can now move on to find out what is the true Church otherwise known as The Body of Christ which exists within the Kingdom of God. So who and where is The Body of Christ?

The Body of Christ is made up of people who:-

- Recognise Jesus as the Son of the Living God
- Believe He died for their sins on the cross of Calvary and on the third day rose again
- Have realised they are a sinner and need to repent
- Have surrendered their lives to Him and received Him into their hearts
- Have been baptised (immersed) in water making a public confession of their faith
- Are filled with the Holy Spirit
- Follow Him by reading and obeying His Word, the Holy Bible and have a personal relationship with Him
- Love, fellowship and care for other believers

It is having a relationship with Jesus Christ not being in religion that defines the people who really make up the true Church. They have a Relationship not a Religion and these believers are all over the world.

In Paul's letter to the Corinthian Church he explains to them how the Body of Christ is structured and how it should function as it is led by the Holy Spirit. He tells them there is only one body and one Spirit and that Christ is the head of the whole body. Read, 1 Corinthians chapter 12.

Once we understand that it is one body made up of many parts and each part is different we can begin to ask the Lord this question. What is my place within your body, Jesus? We have to really understand this part of Scripture and seek to find where we belong.

This has been a hard lesson for me as I expected everyone to want to do the things that I did. I never understood why they didn't. Well here it is - we are all different, we all have a different part to play to make up the whole Body. Our Heavenly Father however, wants us each to be in conjunction and to synchronize with the other parts. *"But now God has set the members every one of them in the body, as it has pleased Him."* 1 Corinthians 12:18

For proper functioning it is crucial that we recognise that it is God and He alone, that has placed us where He wants us to be and not desire another's position or a position that appears greater than where we're at.

Paul further explains in verse 21: *"The eye cannot say to the hand 'I have no need of you' and the head cannot say to the feet, 'I don't need you."* Paul actually exhorts us to give more honour to the innermost parts that to us appear weaker and that the innermost parts are the most precious.

When we take a look at the human body in detail it is not just made up of bones and organs but also has trillions of cells that cannot be externally seen but they are vital. These trillions of cells are the fundamental units of life.

"Look at a beaker of blood, for example, and you'll find that the red blood cells are packed tight. If you used their density to estimate the cells in a human body, you'd come to a staggering 724 trillion cells. Skin cells, on the other hand, are so sparse that they'd give you a paltry estimate of 35 billion cells." [6]

Each part of the human body needs every other part to co-exist and function together. *"We are fearfully and wonderfully made,"* Psalm 139.

---

[6] https://www.smithsonianmag.com/smart-news/there-are-372-trillion-cells-in-your-body-4941473/

When the Body of Christ takes care of itself there is tremendous unity just like the human body. When we esteem others more highly than ourselves then we are on our way to Holy Spirit Unity. Romans 12 and Psalm 133 speak of unity among God's people. Where the brethren dwell in unity there the Lord commands the blessing.

When you have an injury in your own body, or an operation on a certain part, your whole body is affected. This was brought home to me after having an operation on my right hand. I was unable to use it for weeks and this put twice as much strain on my other hand, not only that, my whole body was affected. I could not bend my arm; I could not dress myself properly and needed help. I could not iron (that was good though), I could not drive. That operation, although necessary, took away an awful lot of joy, freedom and independence that I normally have. I remember thinking of this chapter during this period in my life and it really helped me to understand more about the Body of Christ. When one part suffers all the parts suffer and it is so important for us to help one another in our infirmities.

"For He Himself is our peace who has made both one and has broken down the middle wall of separation. Having abolished in His flesh the enmity, that is the law of commandments contained in ordinances so as to create One new man from the two, thus making peace, and that He might reconcile them both to God in one body through the cross." Ephesians 2:4

"...for you were bought with a price therefore glorify God in your body, and in your spirit which are God's." 1 Corinthians 6:20

The Body of Christ has been bought with a price, the precious blood of Jesus, so we are exhorted, *"Let nothing be done through selfish ambition or conceit, but in lowliness of mind let each esteem others better than himself."* Philippians 2:3

"Now, therefore, you are no longer strangers and foreigners, but fellow citizens with the saints and members of the household of God, having been built on the foundation of the apostles and prophets, Jesus Christ Himself being the chief cornerstone, in whom the whole building, being fitted together, grows into a holy temple in the Lord, in whom you also are being built together for a dwelling place of God in the Spirit." Ephesians 2:19-22

It is quite clear from Scripture that all those who belong to Jesus are part of His single body. The members of the body come together, are held together and grow up together all through the work of the Holy Spirit. It is man that continually separates himself from the Body of Christ through wrong doctrine, lack of love for his brethren, thinking himself better than others or because they have received some 'new revelation' to name but a few reasons. If you take a piece of coal out of a fire it will cool down and eventually be cold, it needs other pieces of coal to rekindle it again. The worst thing we can do is isolate ourselves from the Body of Christ.

Some of our behaviour can grieve the Holy Spirit thus causing division. (We will look at this in a later chapter.) I can say, to my shame, that in my walk with Jesus I have sometimes grieved Him too, especially through criticising and judging. I have had to repent of these. What a relief when God forgives you and enables you to continue to walk with Him. It is only through the Word of God and receiving it for yourself that we overcome and the Holy Spirit comes in and helps us.

One passage of Scripture that is very relevant to the body is found in Proverbs 6:16 and states: *"There are 6 things that the Lord hates yes 7 are an abomination;*

- *A proud look*
- *A lying tongue*
- *Hands that shed innocent blood*
- *A heart that devises wicked plans*
- *Feet that are swift to do evil*
- *A false witness that speaks lies*
- <u>*And one who sows discord amongst the brethren."*</u>

God hates disunity so why would we want to do anything that displeases the Lord and causes Him upset? When we are born again and enter into the Body of Christ and the family of God we have a personal responsibility not only to each other but to God Himself to endeavour to keep the bond of unity through the Spirit of peace. We can have amazing peace once we understand that we play an important role in our service to God. Remember there are many, many movements/ religions but there is only one BODY OF CHRIST.

"Endeavouring to keep the unity of the Spirit in the bond of peace. There is one body, and one Spirit, even as ye are called in one hope of your calling; One Lord, one faith, one baptism, One God and Father of all, who is above all, and through all, and in you all." Ephesians 4: 3-6

"For by one Spirit we were all baptized into one body-whether Jews or Greeks, whether slaves or free-and have all been made to drink into one Spirit." 1 Corinthians 12:13

One Body Many Parts

There is only one body with many parts and you are part of that body when you become born again and placed there by God Himself as He pleases. Just as in the Human body, you cannot be part of the Body of Christ and not play your part but, just as the body's cells recycle constantly and disposes of refuse it does not need, so does the Body of Christ. Jesus said: *"Every branch in Me that does not bear fruit He takes away; and every branch that bears fruit He prunes, that it may bear more fruit. Abide in Me, and I in you. As the branch cannot bear fruit of itself, unless it abides in the vine, neither can you, unless you abide in me."*

"I am the vine, you are the branches. He who abides in Me, and I in him, bears much fruit; for without Me you can do nothing. If anyone does not abide in Me, he is cast out as a branch and is withered; and they gather them and throw them into the fire, and they are burned." John 15:2-6

In 1 Corinthians Paul lists the parts of the body and makes it clear there is only One Holy Spirit that works in us all, for the profit of all. He repeats this again in chapter 12:13 *"...for by one Spirit we were all baptized into One Body, whether Jews or Greeks, whether slave or free and have all been made to drink into one spirit. For in fact the body is not one member but many."*

Notice he includes himself. He is not an exclusive apostle; he himself is a member of the Body of Christ in the Kingdom of God. I love verse 23 that states, *"And those members who we think to be less honorable, on those we bestow greater honor and our unpresentable parts have greater modesty."*

"Don't you know that you yourselves are God's temple and that God's Spirit lives in you If anyone destroys God's temple God will destroy him; for God's temple is sacred and you are that temple."
1 Corinthians 3:16

I trust that you can now finally see the True Body of Christ, the True Church that functions in relationships together and not as a ritualistic religion.

Chapter 7

Keeping the Unity of the Spirit

When a person surrenders their heart to Jesus they find out how exciting it is to have a relationship with Him and to know of His love. If you were like me I wanted to do so much to serve Him that sometimes I went overboard trying to repay Him. Which I found out is of course not possible. There is nothing as valuable as the blood of Jesus Christ, nothing we have that can come near to that kind of sacrificial cost.

On a personal note I just wanted to do anything that would please Him, He was and still is real to me and as I heard in a song from my younger days 'He gets sweeter as the days go by' (Gaither Vocal Band and other artists) and that is so true. The Lyrics are worth printing for your enjoyment:-

> The more I trust Him, the more I love Him
> Nothing good for me He'll deny
> The longer I know Him, the better I can show Him
> I couldn't stop now if I tried
> It gets sweeter as the days go by

It gets sweeter as the moments fly

His love is richer, deeper, fuller, sweeter

Sweeter, sweeter, sweeter as the days go by

I eventually realised that I could serve Him best when I found my place in the Body of Christ.

So far we have discovered that religion and relationship are completely different and some religions say they are Christian when in fact they are not, they just use the right words and sometimes in the wrong places. The Holy Spirit is a discerner of hearts and He knows those who truly belong to Christ.

Paul the apostle, seems to be the one that mostly teaches on these matters. In the book of Ephesians he talks about unity and how to walk in that attitude of unity by endeavouring to keep the 'bond of peace' (a commitment to a peace that will preserve our unity). Paul is telling the Ephesians of his mission to the Gentiles (anyone who is not Jewish). Paul himself is a Jewish man, a Pharisee amongst Pharisees (religious leaders) and a Roman citizen. Paul used his status as both a Jew and a Roman citizen to his advantage in ministering to both audiences. According to writings in the New Testament Paul was his Roman name but his Jewish name was Saul of Tarsus. Acts 9:11 and 22:6 In Romans chapters 11 and 12 Paul explains to the Gentiles about being grafted into the vine.

"I beseech you therefore, brethren, by the mercies of God that you present your bodies as a living sacrifice, holy, acceptable unto God which is your reasonable service." Chapter 12:1

This is a wonderful chapter teaching us how to live within the Body of Christ. I love verse 10; *"Be kindly affectioned one to another with brotherly love; in honour preferring one another."*

Paul exhorts the Church to wait upon their ministry; to be content with what the Lord wants us to do, to rejoice together and above all to endeavour to keep the spirit of unity through the bond of peace. Ephesians 4:3

Over my 42 years as a Christian I am ashamed to say I have seen much division. This is caused by the 'leader syndrome' of those who do not have the servant heart as Jesus taught us. The Holy Spirit is truly grieved as we bring worldly programmes, music and ideas into the body and call it Church. The world seems to have gotten into the Church rather than the Church in the world. Please do not misunderstand me, there is room for new resources to be used, especially in the form of technology, but the Holy Spirit has been left out at the expense of some technology.

We need the gift of the discerning of Spirits more than ever before in the life of the Church. If it looks good and sounds good and it makes you feel good …it must be God, seems to be the order of the day.

I can remember times of going to a meeting and as we entered the room someone might be singing a song, from the Spirit, just quietly. Then someone else would pick it up and before long we were in a unified spiritual praise to God. Somehow it would run in line with what the minister subsequently preached and we would all go out amazed, fed and watered by the Holy Spirit Himself. That rarely happens today as we have a programme and a timetable and only those on the platform can speak or sing, there is not much room for the Holy Spirit, if any.

I was really blessed to be part of a worship team for many years, as it is in my heart to worship. Because I was quite shy at praying out loud

I found that some of the songs were like prayers for me, they were written in the Holy Spirit so it was easier for me to sing publicly. Songs like, Create In Me A Clean Heart, Purify My Heart, Draw Me Close To You, Search Me O God, Be Still For The Presence Of The Lord and many more that seemed to make you aware of God's presence. It is in His presence that we do business with God and He speaks to us.

We have a greater job than just attending the Church, we have to endeavour to keep the unity of the Spirit through the bond of peace. In Matthew Jesus says, *"blessed are the peacemakers for they shall become the sons of God."* We have a very real enemy that is called the accuser of the brethren, we see his end in Revelation 12:10.

"Then I heard a loud voice saying in heaven, 'Now salvation, and strength, and the kingdom of our God, and the power of His Christ have come, for the accuser of our brethren, who accused them before our God day and night, has been cast down.'" As satan is the accuser of the brethren he is working everyday to destroy the unity of the Body of Christ.

Peace and blessedness by the Holy Spirit are what brings and keeps the unity in the Body of Christ. Jesus says, *"In me you will have peace."* The Holy Spirit will always back you up when you are trying to do the right thing from your heart that is in line with God's Word, especially where people are willing to forgive. Jesus says that if we do not forgive we will not be forgiven and I think you will agree with me that it is easier said than done. That has been my own experience. All of us at some time or another have done and said things that brought disunity, let us not deceive ourselves into thinking we have not or could not. We are all capable so we need to keep our eyes on Jesus, always reading the Word of God and continuing in fellowship with one another.

None of us can afford to carry around unforgiveness for anyone, especially our brethren, if we want to be an effective part of the Body of Christ. Unforgiveness does not bring peace in our lives or unity in the body. So before we pray and fellowship together we should put things right with each other.

In Mark 11:25 Jesus says, *"And whenever you stand praying, if you have anything against anyone, forgive him, that your Father in heaven may also forgive you your trespasses. But if you do not forgive, neither will your Father in heaven forgive your trespasses."*

In Matthew 5:22-24, Jesus gives practical advice to anyone holding something against their brother, *"But I say to you that whoever is angry with his brother without a cause shall be in danger of the judgment. And whoever says to his brother, 'Raca!' shall be in danger of the council. But whoever says, 'You fool!' shall be in danger of hell fire. Therefore if you bring your gift to the altar, and there remember that your brother has something against you, leave your gift there before the altar, and go your way. First be reconciled to your brother, and then come and offer your gift."*

If there is someone you need to forgive please take heed and do it today, they may not have tomorrow, neither may you.

In the previous chapter we saw how God hates dissension and disunity and that alone should motivate us to keep the unity of the Spirit. Paul's letter to the Church at Ephesus has much to say about keeping the unity of the faith, below are a few verses from chapter 4 verses 25-32 *"'Let each one of you speak truth with his neighbor,' for we are members of one another. 'Be angry, and do not sin': do not let the sun go down on your wrath, nor give place to the devil. Let him who stole steal no longer, but rather let him labor, working with his hands what is good, that he may have something to give him who has need. Let no corrupt word proceed out of your mouth, but what is good for necessary edification, that it may impart grace to the hearers. And do not grieve the Holy Spirit of God, by whom you were sealed for the day of redemption. Let all bitterness, wrath, anger, clamor, and evil speaking be put away from you, with all malice. And be kind to one another, tenderhearted, forgiving one another, even as God in Christ forgave you.*" May I suggest this is a good chapter to study.

A good habit to get into is to encourage one another by texting a word of Scripture or e-mailing something of God's Word that will uplift and edify. Have you ever had a moment when a brother or sister have sent you a little word from God and it was just what you needed at that time? I have and it is wonderful to receive knowing God cares and so do they. It is up to us to keep the peace with everyone and to walk in a spirit of forgiveness, this is the will of God in Christ Jesus. There are many Scriptures to help us but I end this chapter with a command from Jesus Himself...

"*A new commandment I give to you, that you love one another; as I have loved you, that you also love one another.*" John 13:34

Chapter 8

The Gifts are for Today

Are the gifts of the Holy Spirit for today? This question, requires much further study than I am able to write within a few pages. I have looked into many cults and movement over the years that claim many things and it is always the gifts of the Holy Spirit that seem to give them a problem. There are also many Christians who believe some or even all of the gifts are not for today. Personally, I find that difficult to believe having experienced and witnessed most of them. Jesus said, *"I will build My church, and the gates of hell will not prevail against it."* Matthew 16:18

Jesus Is Alive and building His Church or why then did He give some to be apostles, prophets, evangelists, teachers and pastors, for the equipping of the Church, for the work of the ministry?" He also prophesied in Mark 16:14-18 *"Later He appeared to the eleven as they sat at the table; and He rebuked their unbelief and hardness of heart, because they did not believe those who had seen Him after He had risen. And He said to them, 'Go into all the world and preach the gospel to every creature. He who believes and is baptized will be saved; but he who does not believe will be condemned. And these signs will follow those who believe: In My name they will cast out demons; they will speak with new tongues; they will take up serpents; and if they drink anything deadly, it will by no means hurt them; they will lay hands on the sick, and they will recover."'*

Peter states in chapter 2:5 *"...you also, as living stones, are being built up a spiritual house, a holy priesthood, to offer up spiritual sacrifices acceptable to God through Jesus Christ."*

On reading this it tells me that we are all still being built up in the Holy Spirit so we can worship in Spirit and in Truth. The gifts are given for the building of the Church.

There are 1000's of testimonies of Christians still being baptised in the Holy Spirit. How then has He ceased? I think it is because of fear, that so many deny Him because they cannot see or understand Him through human reasoning. Which leads you to wonder if they really do know Him although they say they are born again and filled with Him? It just doesn't add up, does it?

Anyone who tells you that the Holy Spirit ceased with the apostles is committing a spiritual crime and my advice is to flee from them, it is heresy.[7] If Jesus is not building His Church through the power of the Holy Spirit that means that man is. *"I say again, 'it is not by might nor by power but by my Spirit says the Lord'"* Zechariah 4:6

Below is a paragraph taken from Watchtower 2000 website:-

[7] Belief or opinion contrary to orthodox religious (especially Christian) doctrine. (Oxford Dictionary)

At that time, such "powerful works" were provided to show that the fledgling Christian congregation had God's backing. (Hebrews 2:4) But after having served their purpose, they would be "done away with," said the apostle Paul. (1 Corinthians 13:8) Thus, we do not now observe in the true Christian congregation any God-ordained healings, prophetic messages, or the exorcising of demons.[8]

They have conveniently left out the next sentence in 1 Corinthians 13, *"For we know in part and we prophesy in part. But when that which is perfect has come, then that which is in part will be done away."* Only when He (Jesus) that is perfect comes will they cease as we will not need the gifts, we will have Jesus. This is just one example of twisting Scripture to say the gifts are done away with. My mother-in-law never spoke to us for 10 years, when we became Christians, after she joined the Jehovah's Witnesses.

They taught her that we were children of the devil because we spoke in tongues. Not to mention that the many healings that I had experienced made me off limits to her. Needless to say my children really missed out on a grandmother and we lost 10 years of family life with her. Just to say that she did accept Jesus as her Saviour during her last few days on earth. Praise God! There are so many more erroneous groups you can research for yourself because this kind of false teaching is prevalent today.

Some Christian churches do not believe in the Holy Spirit in a believer's life either. They believe that we just have to try and be better people. Well, you can try all you want, many people make new year resolutions and most never make it past 6 weeks because it is a man made thing. It is only with the power of the Holy Spirit that we can change to become more like Jesus.

---

[8] https://wol.jw.org/en/wol/d/r1/lp-e/2000242

If you should do your own research you will find many churches do not or will not operate in the gifts of the Spirit. People become believers because they want to feel different, they want hope and love and acceptance in their lives. They want to see powerful demonstrations that Jesus is alive and the Helper that He promised to send is indeed at work amongst them. It is the full gospel of Jesus Christ that is the power of God unto salvation. Paul says, *"For I am not ashamed of the gospel of Christ, for it is the power of God to salvation for everyone who believes, for the Jew first and also for the Greek."* Romans 1:16

There are many cults like the Jehovah's Witnesses and other denominations that deny the power and person of the Holy Spirit. Some preach that if you say the sinner's prayer you are saved forever and can continue to live the life you want. That is not what the Bible teaches even Peter stood up on the day of Pentecost and replied to the crowd when they cried out, *"What must we do to be saved?"* He said, *"Repent, be baptised everyone of you and you shall receive the gift of the Holy Spirit."* Well, I think that's clear don't you?

Peter, a disciple of the Lord who had practically lived alongside Jesus during His time on the earth. Peter, who was once a fisherman out on the stormy seas, who was called by Jesus Himself. This is the same Peter that stood up! Some will never acknowledge that the Holy Spirit is a person. That it is He who helps us to pursue the Kingdom of God with the gifts that have been so graciously given. In the book of Joel, Joel prophesied saying, *"In the last days I will pour out My Spirit on ALL flesh. Your sons and your daughters will prophesy."* Joel 2:27 Are we not still in the last days?

We know we are in the last days as this prophecy of the pouring out of God's Spirit was fulfilled at Pentecost. God, by His Spirit, continues the work of the Kingdom through all true believers until we are called home to be with Jesus. We also know from reading about the person of the Holy Spirit that He is a very important and tangible part of the Godhead. That His gifts are very real and needed too, and so are the ministry gifts of Jesus, through which, God can manifest His power and His glory. We also know that Jesus is building His Church through born again believers who are full of the Holy Spirit. John chapter 3

We have previously addressed some of those who claim that the gifts went out when all the original prophets died, hmmm! Well, there were 3,000 born again at Pentecost and filled with the Spirit speaking in a new language. I wonder what happened to them? The apostle Paul was constantly seeking new believers and wanting them to receive the Holy Spirit and just to mention, Paul was not one of the original 12 disciples. He was not there at Pentecost. His conversion experience was so different and so filled with the demonstration of God's power and it makes very worthwhile, exciting and interesting reading. See Acts Chapter 8

One of the most controversial gifts is 'tongues' but in Mark 16, it is the resurrected Jesus that gives the prophecy of speaking in new tongues. Yes, we need to be discerning, yes we have to ensure that we have the truth of God's Word but let us stop listening to all these myths and start to ask the Holy Spirit to teach us and also to read our own Bibles for ourselves in context. Let us stop relying on other people's opinions thoughts and ideas and let us keep our eyes on Jesus, the author and finisher of our faith. Let us not be lazy at researching the Bible for ourselves. Let us have a love for God and His Word and a love for one another to see the Kingdom of God extended. The truth is simple and clear, Paul warns us...

"Oh, that you would bear with me in a little folly-and indeed you do bear with me. For I am jealous for you with godly jealousy. For I have

betrothed you to one husband, that I may present you as a chaste virgin to Christ. But I fear, lest somehow, as the serpent deceived Eve by his craftiness, so your minds may be corrupted from the simplicity that is in Christ. For if he who comes preaches another Jesus whom we have not preached, or if you receive a different spirit which you have not received, or a different gospel which you have not accepted-you may well put up with it." 2 Corinthians 11:1-4

The apostle Paul spent a great deal of his time teaching on the gifts and showing the Churches how to operate in an orderly manner so we can learn from one another. *"How is it then, brethren? Whenever you come together, each of you has a psalm, has a teaching, has a tongue, has a revelation, has an interpretation. Let all things be done for edification. If anyone speaks in a tongue, let there be two or at the most three, each in turn, and let one interpret. But if there is no interpreter, let him keep silent in Church, and let him speak to himself and to God. Let two or three prophets speak, and let the others judge. But if anything is revealed to another who sits by, let the first keep silent. For you can all prophesy one by one, that all may learn and all may be encouraged. And the spirits of the prophets are subject to the prophets. For God is not the author of confusion but of peace, as in all the churches of the saints."* Acts 14 26-33

You can find really good teaching on the different cults and religions that will help you to dispel these myths that have crept into Christianity. We have a very real enemy in the devil and he loves to distort the truth. He also knows his own destiny and he wants to take as many with him as possible to an eternity without God, called hell. *"Be self-controlled and alert. Your enemy the devil prowls around like a roaring lion looking for someone to devour. Resist him standing firm in the faith."* 1 Peter 5:8 (NIV)

Understand that where the Holy Spirit is the devil always sends a counterfeit, so we are exhorted to be submissive to one another and be clothed in humility; *"...for 'God resists the proud but gives grace to the humble.' Therefore humble yourselves under the mighty hand of God, that He may exalt you in due time, casting all your cares on Him for He cares for you."* 1 Peter 5:5-7

When you are filled with the Holy Spirit He enables you to carry out the work of the Kingdom and the devil does not like you. The devil also masquerades as an angel of light so we can easily be deceived. That is why we need the gift of discerning spirits, to understand that the Word of God in us and working in our lives, is the most powerful weapon in our arsenal against him.

There is no account in Scripture of the Holy Spirit ceasing to be poured out. How else will Jesus build His Church/His Body except through the power and gifts of the Holy Spirit. As far as I know, Jesus IS STILL building His Church. It says in Ephesians 2:22 *"...in whom you also are being built together for a dwelling place of God in the Spirit."*

This is present continuous tense as in an ongoing work. The Bible is the most powerful, living and wonderful book for our lives, let us not look to man for the Truth or we will be blown around by every wind of doctrine. Let us look to Jesus the Author and Finisher of our faith as He is the Way, the Truth and the Life.

Chapter 9

Manifestation of Gifts within the Body

The whole reason for writing this book is that I have found many Christians ignorant of the Holy Spirit and His enabling power called also His unction/anointing. God's Word says that He does not want us to be ignorant; so unless you are prepared to read the Word of God and invest time into trying to understand it you never really will get the full understanding. I would like to add here that only the Holy Spirit will reveal God's Word to us as He is the Author of it. It amazes me how many Christians do not understand the fulfilment of Christ's work here on earth. He said He came to fulfil the law and the prophets but unless we read the Old Testament to find out about the law and the prophets we can never understand what He has fulfilled in the New Testament.

For example, we would not understand why He was called 'The Lamb of God that takes away the sins of the World' or what He was talking about when He cried from the cross, *"It is finished."* And yet these are very basic to our Christianity. Please, my friend, if you are reading this may I implore you to spend time with God in His Word (if you don't already) and ask Him questions and if you are unsure then seek out wise counsel, people full of the Word and of the Holy Spirit.

During my time in Christian Ministry, I have been used by the Holy Spirit to demonstrate most of the gifts and I have also seen terrible misuse and ungodly behaviour in the name of the Holy Spirit. I pray that during these next few chapters I can share some insight that will help you to use the gifts God has given you. I cannot go any further though without mentioning FAITH, BECAUSE WITHOUT FAITH IT IS IMPOSSIBLE TO PLEASE GOD. No matter what gift we have it takes faith to use it. Faith is always obedience to God and His Word. If you are in any doubt regarding what God has said to you it is very easy to gain assurance. Our measuring rod is God's Word alone. If what we hear does not line up with the Word of God then it is not God. That is why it is imperative that we know the Word or how else can we discern the truth of the instruction/inspiration that we have heard? The written Word/the Bible always has the priority and the last word.

At this point I just want to say that a safeguard is to earnestly desire Jesus (Yeshua, Messiah) more than His gifts or anything else for that matter. Get to know Him and His presence in a deeper way. That is more important than anything. I have been told that there were many men in that day named Jesus and my reply to them is there is only one Jesus CHRIST that rose from the dead. The others are still in the grave.

*****

Spiritual Gifts

What is a Gift?

A gift is something we give to someone usually at birthdays and special occasions and consider it a pleasure to do so. How difficult it is sometimes to receive a gift though? There is a Bible passage that says, *"...it is more blessed to give than to receive;"* and that is not because it is easier to give than to receive. It is actually harder because it costs us more money, effort, thought and so on. We are complicated human beings however, so although it is easier to receive, for many of us, our pride will not allow us to accept anything from others.

I love thinking of someone to buy a gift for. What they might like or even better what they might need. To shop around for it and suddenly find the perfect item, just for them, brings me great pleasure. I get so happy when I see their face, when they open it up and it is exactly what they wanted or had need of. The hugs and kisses that go with that memorable moment, are priceless, especially those from my children and grandchildren.

For me, to receive a gift has taken years of understanding the pleasure it gives the giver. This was notable one Christmas when my grandchildren, that live in Australia, were over for the holidays. They had asked my husband, what he thought I would like for Christmas and had carefully shopped around for it. My son Rob obviously purchased it for them but oh, the delight and surprise I felt when I opened that gift and found a brand new Laptop. The look on their faces was wonderful as they saw my delight and surprise. That was a moment I will always treasure.

Imagine then how God feels when His children receive the good gifts that He offers to them and imagine how He would feel if it is rejected. *"If a son shall ask bread of any of you that is a father, will he give him a stone? Or if he ask for a fish, will he give him a serpent, or if he shall ask for an egg, will he offer him a scorpion? If you then, being evil, know how to give good gifts to your children: how much more shall your Heavenly Father give the Holy Spirit to them that ask him?"* Luke 11:11-13

What is a Spiritual Gift?

The word 'gift' in Corinthians means charisma, grace, favor and kindness. (Young's Analytical Concordance) So God bestows and gives us these gifts out of His amazing act of grace, favor and kindness. They are for His purposes alone and to bring glory to Him. We cannot earn them or buy them as Simon the sorcerer found out. You can read about Simon in Acts chapter 8.

For the gifts and the calling of God are irrevocable [for He does not withdraw what He has given, nor does He change His mind about those to whom He gives His grace or to whom He sends His call]. Romans 11:9 (Amplified Version). This version puts it so much better than I could.

When you give a gift to someone you never ask for it back, you have given it willingly and with joy. What they do with that gift is nothing to do with us once it is given. It is for them to decide.

In the Spiritual realm it is not like that. Although given with love and joy the gift given by God is for His use for building up the Body of Christ. He trusts us not to misuse these divine gifts, to listen to Him Tell us when to use them and to activate our faith in believing that they are for that particular time.

We cannot be in the Body of Christ and not function in a particular part. There is no fence to sit on, you are either in or out of His body. You either have the gift of the Holy Spirit or not. We cannot function without Him. We need His unction to function as a whole.

We cannot see inside of our body but we know by faith that the heart and lungs etc. are working. We cannot see the trillions of cells but we know they are at work keeping us healthy. I cannot explain to you how our eyes work in detail but I know they are working because I can see. I think you know where I am coming from. The Body of Christ is alive and well because it is the Holy Spirit that unites true believers. He inspires the different parts to bring glory to God through their actions. *"Now the Lord is that Spirit, and where the Spirit of the Lord is, there is liberty."* 2 Corinthians 3:17

What I am trying to say is, we do not see everything the Lord is doing and because we do not always understand the enemy tries to deceive us by pointing fingers and being negative about the Kingdom of God. I have heard it so many times: "Oh nothing is happening… where is God?" "There used to be such power in the meetings." "The Holy Spirit has left us" etc. Jesus said He would be with us forever that He would not leave us as orphans and either we believe that or we do not. I choose to believe the words of Jesus. He will abide with you forever.

There are manifestations of the Holy Spirit and there are special gifts given by Jesus to equip and build up the body, we will look at these in another chapter.

There are nine gifts that manifest the power of the Holy Spirit within a believer and I will put them into classification for ease of reading. 1 Corinthians 12:4-11 is where you can read about these gifts. If you can, read all of 1 Corinthians chapters 12 to 14.

Gifts of Power:
- Faith
- Working of Miracles
- Healings

Gifts of Revelation:
- Word of Wisdom

- Word of Knowledge
- Discerning of Spirits

Gifts of Inspiration:
- Prophecy
- Divers kinds of Tongues
- Interpretation of Tongues

In chapter 12:7, Paul states *"...but the manifestation of the Spirit is given to each one for the profit of all."*

No gift is given for ourselves it is for the body. Every one of the above gifts from God can only operate through faith believing that the Lord has spoken. Because the Holy Spirit is a person and a gentleman He does not force His way into our lives and make us do things. The Spirit is subject to the prophet. In other words when God speaks we either obey (faith) or ignore Him. He still gives us that choice so we can never say, "I could not help it."

These gifts are not to make us feel good or boast that we are someone special. There are many other gifts too, for example the gift of hospitality or administration. Can you list more?

As mentioned earlier, there is an account of Simon the Sorcerer that when he saw the apostles working amazing miracles he considered purchasing this gift from Peter.

"And when Simon saw that through laying on of the apostles' hands the Holy Ghost was given, he offered them money, saying: 'Give me also this power, that on whomsoever I lay hands, he may receive the Holy Ghost.' But Peter said unto him, "Thy money perish with thee, because thou hast thought that the gift of God may be purchased with money. Thou hast

neither part nor lot in this matter, for thy heart is not right in the sight of God." Acts chapter 8:14-21

All the gifts are exactly what the word says, A GIFT.

"For by grace you have been saved through faith, and that not of yourselves; it is the gift of God, not of works, lest anyone should boast." Ephesians 2:8-9 The gifts of the Spirit are like that too. By grace God imparts to whom He wishes. We cannot earn our salvation and we cannot buy gifts in the Kingdom. It is all by the Grace of God for the building of His Kingdom. It's all about HIM.

Gifts of Power

"Now concerning spiritual gifts, brethren, I do not want you to be ignorant:." 1 Corinthians 12:1
As stated before the gifts of power are Faith, Working of Miracles and Gifts of Healing.

Faith:
This is one of the most confusing gifts. Many will say 'I have got Faith' but the faith that they are talking about is Faith IN God. True faith believes that God is who He says He is. Romans 10:17 says, *"Faith cometh by hearing and hearing by the Word of God."* Reading the Bible builds our faith. The more we read the more we will believe in God and who He is, so we have a witness in our spirit that the Word is true.
"All Scripture is given by inspiration of God and is profitable for reproof for doctrine for correction and for training in righteousness, that the man of God may be complete thoroughly equipped for every good work." 2 Timothy chapter 3:16

Faith is very important. Jesus was concerned and once questioned whether He would find any faith in the earth when He returns.

It is in 1 Corinthians chapter 12 that Paul speaks about the 'gift' of faith. This is a complete trust in God when He has spoken to us personally through His Word (there are other ways the Holy Spirit can speak to us). This is an inner prompting not necessarily an audible voice although it certainly can be, it is up to God. Believing what God says to you is the first step and then when you act upon it, this is the second step, obedience. Smith Wigglesworth's famous quote says: "God says it; I believe it and that settles it." Amen. Not much room for discussion there then.

It is not a 'name it and claim it' doctrine. It will be for a situation that may be personal to you that you have been praying about and only you and God know about it. You act upon it in faith and it brings success and above all glory to God because you now have a testimony of that situation. So the gift of faith is a specific word given for a specific need that empowers you to deal with the situation and is different from the everyday trust you have in God.

Working of Miracles:
This actually means power or powers and we must remember here that it is God's power not ours. We have no special powers except the wonderful power that faith can release when activated. In Acts 19 we read of some amazing things that Paul actually did and it says he worked unusual miracles so that even handkerchiefs or aprons were brought to the sick and diseases left them (verse 12) and the evil spirits went out of them. I personally believe that Paul had the faith to believe God to use those items. Maybe God had told him to do it, we do not know, all we know is that this action would have required faith.

James tells us in chapter 5:14-16 that if there is anyone among you that is sick to call for the elders of the Church and let them pray over you with oil and in the name of Jesus, and that the prayer of faith will save the sick and the Lord will raise them up. Also if they have committed any sins they will be forgiven. This is faith and obedience in action by both parties. When we ask these things with wrong motives (e.g. self-adulation, seeking a good reputation, to look good or jealousy) we ask wrongly. Even though God can and will work despite us, we need to ask these things with pure motives to bring glory to God.

The greatest Miracle Worker of all time is Jesus Himself and we read many accounts in the gospels, but let us not forget He is alive and working miracles through His Body/Church today. Jesus said, *"Verily, verily, I say unto you, He that believeth on me, the works that I do shall he do also; and greater works than these shall he do; because I go unto my Father."* John 14:12

Healing:

I have personally received many miracles including healings from Jesus but they have always come through His Word mixed with my faith. You can read some of them in my little booklet 'Reach for Your Miracle' I have put one of the accounts here below as it demonstrates faith in action followed by a miracle of healing. All three of the gifts working together bringing God glory. My deepest gratitude goes to Him.

No Cure

*****

During this exciting time, not long after being baptised in the Holy Spirit and before we moved to Westhoughton, I began experiencing some terrible nightmares and then one night I awoke and could not move. I tried to speak but nothing came out of my mouth. As I tried to awaken my husband Dennis (now my ex husband) I became afraid as I knew no sound was coming out of my mouth. I eventually made a noise and this awakened him, when he looked at me I could see from his face something was wrong. It felt as though my face was twisted and saliva was coming out of my mouth. With help from Dennis I came round wondering what on earth had happened. All I could think of during this time was Jesus, I knew He was there and it was as if my body was rising to the ceiling towards a bright light. My brain was acutely aware of what was going on – I could hear and understand what Dennis was saying to me but I was unable to respond. Terror struck me.

When I eventually came round I began to cry with relief. I felt exhausted and helpless. A couple of days later I was still exhausted and drained and worried because although this was new to me I was left with a familiar feeling that I could not put my finger on. This was the beginning of an horrific illness and it started to destroy me mentally, physically and emotionally. Jesus had graciously healed me of an arthritic jaw as a new Christian so I knew and had tasted of the goodness of God. All I had to do now was pray and He would heal me…wouldn't He?

These attacks/seizures started to become more frequent so whenever there was an altar call in church I would be the first at the front. Daily in my own prayer life I would ask the Lord to heal me but heaven seemed like brass. I was reading God's Word at every opportunity as I became hungry to know the Jesus who had passionately saved my soul through the shedding of His precious divine blood. We were seeing souls saved in our families and I was even laying hands on the sick, in faith, and Jesus healed them (James 5:13-16).

These seizures were now happening two to three times a week and I was afraid to go to sleep at night as this was when it happened. I was also afraid to tell anyone. I heard well meaning Christians, from the pulpit, preaching that you must be in sin if you are suffering in sickness. I couldn't believe it! This wasn't the God I had read about.

Eventually we went to a doctor, privately, and after many tests I was diagnosed with Nocturnal Epilepsy and Sleeping Paralysis of which, he said, there was NO CURE. I was devastated and desperate. He prescribed some medication and for the first time in a long time I slept peacefully. This peacefulness was not without payment because after three short weeks I knew I had become addicted to the drugs and moreover the seizures returned. At £40 a time I could not afford to return to the doctor. I was now in a worse state than before having seizures and addicted to drugs that were having no positive results. I was still heavily into reading God's Word and praying, believing God would heal me and yet I had the feeling that I must not be a good enough Christian. I felt that I was not doing enough, not worthy enough for God to heal me of this, I became of a mind to take my own life because at thirty five years old, I did not want to live the rest of my life in this condition.

I have always loved Jesus since becoming born again. He introduced me to a life of faith, fun and a future in Him and the longer I served Him the sweeter He grew. I used to say, 'only if this is for the glory of God can I endure'. This went on for five years.

One Saturday night I had a terrible seizure and on the Sunday morning I was exhausted and wanted to stay in bed. Dennis would normally leave me to sleep it off but this morning was different he encouraged me to try to get up so we could go to church. He said it was the best place for me to be. We arrived late and sat at the back and towards the end of the meeting I sensed the Holy Spirit say to me, "Ask the elders to lay hands on you." In the other ear came a response "You've done that a few times but it hasn't worked has it?" Well, I know which voice is in the word of God and it wasn't that one. The Bible says, *"obedience is better than sacrifice"*, 1 Samuel 15:25 so after the meeting I asked Willie Hacking, a dear friend of Smith Wigglesworth and a Godly saint to pray for me. People were busy coming and going and Mr Hacking had no idea what was wrong with me, he didn't need to, God knew. He prayed a simple prayer of faith and I went home.

There were no flashing lights or clashes of thunder JUST FAITH. After all, I had asked for prayer so many times why should this be any different? As the day moved on and bedtime approached I reached for my tablets when I heard a still small voice (not audible) in my spirit, say these words "trust me Barbara". That's the first time I remember God calling me by my name and at that moment looking back I had a choice yet again to listen to God or carry on doing what I had been doing, taking my medication. I decided to trust the Lord after all, if I died through one of these seizures I would win and if I lived I would win. From that day to this I stand as a testimony to the greatness of God and His healing power in the 21st century. I HAVE NEVER SUFFERED SINCE and here I am over thirty years later. Once when I was sharing this testimony with someone I said it took five years for God to heal me and the Lord checked me in my spirit saying, "1000 years is but a day to the Lord, I heard you the same day you cried out".

Caution:
I only stopped taking medication because God had spoken to me personally. I do not advocate anyone stopping their medication without their doctor's advice. This was the gift of faith at work.

As you can see from my testimony I did receive a miracle of healing for which I am forever grateful to God and I have told this testimony many, many times and I am sure that God has used it to encourage and heal others over the years. This was very personal too. Healings can happen anywhere and at any time in the Kingdom of God. It does not always happen in church meetings but it can. It still has to come by hearing God through the preaching or reading of His Word.

You may be drawn to someone by the Holy Spirit and God gives you the faith to pray for that person who is sick. If He has given you that word it could be that your faith is being tested or that He is using you to heal that person. Whatever the outcome it is up to God not us. The gift of healing is to help the person who is sick or unwell.

You will have noticed by now that these three gifts of Power usually work in harmony with each other but in each case it depends on us and our obedience as we look to Jesus. In 2 Timothy 3:5 it says; There will be Godlessness in the last days, people will have a form of Godliness but deny the power thereof and we are exhorted to have nothing to do with them. Isn't this true today? There are many cults and movements that use the name of God to validate their existence and to lure men and women into falsehood, so that they cannot see Jesus. The Bible says, *"...the God of this world has blinded their eyes to the truth."* John 12:40

Part of the reason for the lack of effectiveness, in the Church today, I believe, is that God's people are bound up by a fear of allowing the Holy Spirit to operate in their lives and in their congregations.

Gifts of Revelation:

What does revelation mean? It actually means an unveiling or revealing. Something that has been covered or unseen but can now be seen or revealed.

These three manifestations of the Holy Spirit are:
- A Word of Wisdom
- A Word of Knowledge
- Discerning of spirits

Words of Wisdom and Knowledge:

All this revealing comes from God through the Holy Spirit as and when needed. You can receive a word of knowledge by dreaming of a situation or when praying for someone or something in particular. God does speak to us but we need to believe what He tells us. It is easier for me to give a few examples which should explain these gifts more clearly and hopefully allow you to put a handle on things that may be happening in your own life presently.

Firstly, we have a choice as to whether we should do something about the situation or not. God always gives us the choice, HE NEVER forces us to do anything against our will.

One of the many incidents in my own life, I remember, is going to church one morning and a young friend announcing that she was pregnant. Immediately the Holy Spirit told me that this was her father's child by sexual abuse. What a shock that was to me. How was I going to handle it? Did I believe it was true? I had never met her father. Somehow I knew it was true and of course having being abused myself I was desperate to be able to put a stop to it. She had a boyfriend at the time and so maintained that it was his baby but I knew it wasn't.

I needed the help of the Holy Spirit, His wisdom and strategy so as not to cause more unnecessary pain, after all this was very serious. To my shame I was not brave enough to confront the young woman so I confided in my husband and we watched the family closely as there were two other girls in the family who could be suffering from the same abuse. In the book of James it states *"...those who lack wisdom let them ask."*

I prayed very hard for wisdom and that God Himself would reveal the situation. That is exactly what happened, thankfully God did reveal the situation and it was an awful time. This father had been abusing all three of his daughters and was eventually arrested, convicted and imprisoned. The strategy God gave me was to pray that it all would be revealed and leave it up to Him. I believe this was the Word of knowledge and wisdom working together for the glory of God and resolution.

How wonderful is the Lord? I am always amazed how He cares for each of us even when in tragic circumstances and how He upholds those who trust Him. Oh how near He is to the broken.

Many years ago I was involved in a fabulous worship team. Our pianist was great at praising the Lord and extremely energetic. There was a real anointing upon him. He was happily married with a son and his wife also sang in the team. We had not realised how much we were all gifted in the Holy Spirit as we loved to worship God together. Of course we very soon came under attack from satan. During this time I discerned that our pianist was having an affair so I took my concerns to our church leaders who had already had their own suspicions. I was not very confident at the time and I did not want to betray anyone or be disloyal but God had revealed it to me through a word of knowledge for a purpose.

Unfortunately, it was later proven to be true. That did not make him a bad person but God will not be mocked we must honour His word and live accordingly.

We cannot be in these positions within the Body of Christ without first being accountable to God who placed us there in the first place. He has said, there is nothing secret that will not be revealed. God is interested in our lives and cares for us very much, after all, He sent His own Son to die for our sins because He loved the whole world. He cared enough for this person to reveal it so he could have an opportunity to repent and move on. Unfortunately, it did not end well and this pianist is no longer in ministry. How sad is that, when will we realise we have a real enemy who is out to steal, kill and destroy us? More importantly that God is a loving and forgiving God who will cleanse and restore when we mess up our lives with sin, as long as we have asked for that forgiveness.

I gave a couple who were our friends, who had been separated, a word from God that they would be reunited on their wedding anniversary even though all seemed lost. The Holy Spirit spoke and they did reconcile on their wedding anniversary and are still together.

During the past few years when praying with a group of women in Rochdale, UK we laid hands on a woman who was having trouble conceiving and the Holy Spirit gave a prophetic word for her that she would conceive and have a baby the following summer. This was an encouraging word but although it was joyous it needed my faith and wisdom to actually speak it out as this was something that could be proved or disproved. The enemy of our souls always brings his favourite tools out in these cases and it is called DOUBT.

The couple had been trying for a baby for a long time and she thought she was barren so it would have been very upsetting for them if I gave them the word and it did not happen. This would also bring the Body of Christ into disrepute. Within a few weeks, we heard the joyous news that she was pregnant and we had the joy of holding that little girl when she was born.

When your concern is for the Kingdom of God and you love the Body of Christ God does not withhold His wonderful gifts from us. I remember going to preach at one church and was horrified when the Lord gave me the word that He had departed from that church because of sin. I had to give it in obedience hoping they would deal with it but they didn't. It was only months later that the church closed. Not all words of knowledge or discerning of spirits are easy to give and you definitely need wisdom in operating in them, as well as the gift of faith.

There are many examples I could give that would take up chapters but I am sure you may have had similar experiences and not realised you have a gift from God. They sometimes bring joy and some bring correction and rebuke but as Paul states in 1 Corinthians 12, nonetheless we should eagerly desire gifts.

When we look in the Bible we can see other accounts of God's knowledge and wisdom imparted to His prophets. Let us look at Nathan the prophet and king David (Samuel chapter 12). God showed Nathan that David had been committing adultery with Bathsheba who was the wife of Uriah. Uriah loved David, protected him and fought for him in his army and was a loyal subject. David sent him on the front line of battle knowing he would be killed and he did this so it would be 'legal' for him to have Bathsheba as his wife. He tried to cover up his sin and was so captivated by her that he did not care at all about the life and well-being of such a dedicated servant. After all, he was king, he could do as he liked and he could have anything he wanted.

It is hard to believe this is the same David who wrote many of the Psalms that still bless us today. The same David who had a heart after God's own heart and loved the Lord. Now, even though he has everything he could ever dream of, he still wants more to the point of coveting another man's wife. The enemy of our souls is always on the lookout for our weaknesses but David here did not consider himself weak because he wore the crown of Israel and Judah. God loved David and gave him another chance by sending the prophet Nathan to warn him to repent. Nathan went in boldness and wisdom to confront David. The wisdom he uses is wonderful and the outcome amazing. It is in the book of 2 Samuel chapter 12.

The book of Acts gives us amazing accounts of how the Holy Spirit gives revelation and knowledge to the Body of Christ. In Acts 5 Peter was given knowledge about Ananias and Sapphira's dishonesty with dire consequences. In chapter 10, Cornelius had a vision and by faith he acted on that vision with the results that he and his household were saved and came to the knowledge of God. In chapter 27, Paul was given a word of knowledge and wisdom when the ship he was on hit a storm and it looked destined to sink with the loss of many lives.

Discerning of Spirits:
Let us look at the actual word discerning. In this context it means a thorough judging (diakrisis) spiritually. Our enemy prowls around like a roaring lion seeking whom he may devour. He comes in all shapes and sizes and can appear very plausible. He is not always nasty and he can come as an angel of light. Discernment is one of the most needed gifts in the Church today.

We need to understand that we are not judging people but the spirit of those people. This can show itself in normal conversation as well as in a Holy Spirit meeting. Ananias and Sapphira told lies to Peter and he discerned they were lying. He had faith enough to tell them they were lying to the Holy Spirit and then prophesied their fate, which of course was death.

I do believe many of us have this but maybe nervous or afraid to use it. We have to realise this gift is for the whole Body of Christ. God can warn us and help us only if we cooperate with Him, realising that it is given for our benefit and protection. We have our human spirit and there are evil spirits and the Holy Spirit and we can only discern evil spirits if we have the Holy Spirit. They are spiritually discerned.

We were at a Christian conference at Cefn Lea in the late 80's when we were asked to join the speaker Mike Ross Watson, who had been a missionary to Jakarta, at the front to pray for people. Well as we began to pray for this woman she fell to the ground, I thought it was the Holy Spirit, but my partner knew it was not and very boldly told her to get up because her falling was not the doing of the Holy Spirit. I felt quite embarrassed but at that moment she began to squirm like a snake and attack him. Fortunately there were plenty of ministers that came to our assistance and the woman was set gloriously free.

My pastor always said that if you go 'down in the Spirit' you should get up differently that there should be a change in you. In your habits and in your personality you should become more like Jesus. There seemed a lot of 'falling down' in those days but I wonder how many were true encounters of the Holy Spirit.

I can think of numerous occasions when I have discerned spirits and in some cases have not asked God for wisdom how to go about it. In other cases it was when I was a young Christian and too afraid to upset others. This is due to a lack of understanding and dare I say a lack of teaching. Another reason for proceeding without wisdom is due to our human nature that wants to be accepted and wants to be approved of and liked. Maybe these are the reasons this gift is not in operation very much today.

In Psalm 133 we have already mentioned that where the brethren dwell in unity there the Lord commands a blessing. Unity is something we all seem to crave for and it is what our Lord wants from us. Our enemy however, is out to destroy, divide and conquer us. We just need to ask ourselves why there are so many divisions within the Body of Christ. I personally have witnessed many in my walk with Jesus and it breaks my heart so, I am sure it breaks His. I have learned that we have to guard our own hearts and be aware of the enemy's tactics. Oh, there is much teaching on this but is there much real learning?

Some of the spirits within the Church today are: - jealousy, selfish ambition, pride, lust, hatred and discord to name a few. I have noticed these are not tangible or something you can easily see but you have to discern them. There is also, I believe, a spirit named after king Ahab's wife Jezebel and although she was a woman this spirit does not always manifest in women. This account of Ahab and Jezebel can be found in the book of Kings. This spirit is not to be taken lightly as it is out to destroy the prophets of God (those who bring the word of direction/growth to the Church). I have experienced this one first hand and I praise God that His protection kept me from being destroyed.

The Body of Christ has to wake up to this particular spirit. If you are in a fellowship that has freedom to operate in the gifts of the Holy Spirit then you should be in a position to speak with your Elders what you have discerned. You then need to pray for wisdom for yourself and the Elders to deal with it. It may need prayer and fasting. Do not try to deal with it on your own, get wise counsel.

The greatest gift that we can desire is love especially when operating in the gifts as God knows the sincerity of our hearts. This too is very important when dealing with someone who needs deliverance/to be set free from evil spirits. (This is a whole other subject on its own.)

Below is an extract from 'Reach for your Miracle' as I know I was truly delivered and set free this particular night, from an evil spirit.

*****

Delivered From Smoking

When I first got saved at Radcliffe Tabernacle AOG (Assemblies of God) Church I was smoking forty cigarettes a day. I would have at least five in the morning along with a pot of tea. I remember visiting the doctor and he told me that, after examining my chest, he would not like to examine me ten years on. I was in my early thirties then. I really didn't take much notice of that, after all, nothing happens to you does it, it happens to other people. Well after my born again experience the urge to smoke left me. I only wish I could say that I didn't start again but I did.

The more I studied God's Word the more convicted I became to give up smoking but I did not find this easy at all. I was getting to the point of paranoia as I knew the Lord wanted me to stop abusing my body. Oh I used to be very opinionated about drug addicts and how they had no will power and how disgusting they were until one day when I was so desperate to stop this smoking I sensed the Lord tell me, "but you are a drug addict." I was shocked but HE WAS RIGHT. Coming to terms with this was awful because I could not give them up.

Knowing God hears and answers prayer I began asking Him to help me as I wanted to be a good witness for Him. Every time I picked up my Bible I would read 'Holiness as unto the Lord' this did not mean because I smoked I was not holy although at the time I thought it did. No, God wanted obedience from me in this matter and I could not do it. I felt so ashamed I was saying I will do anything you ask of me Lord and here I am unable to give up smoking for Him.

Over a six month period I became more and more desperate until one night in our church an appeal was given for people to come out to the front for prayer. I was ashamed to tell anyone that I wanted to give up smoking as I thought they would have seen me as a failure in Jesus and I did not want to let Jesus down. How funny when they must have smelled the nicotine on me. Anyway this night in fear and trembling I went forward for prayer. I managed to tell the pastor that I needed to stop smoking and do you know what? He didn't even pass a comment or seemed perturbed in any way.

As he began to pray for me I felt so sick and desperate before my God that eventually this awful scream came from within me. I was horrified that people had heard me as I was a quiet person back then. I had no idea what had happened to me, I don't think anyone else did either. I know now though. I never suffered any withdrawal symptoms from my forty a day addiction, to this day. God delivered me from this addictive hold on my life that I believe was a demon. I do not want to enter into any theological debates on this or any other part of my testimony, because it is a testimony that when God is present by His Spirit with desperate souls HE HEARS THEIR CRIES and delivers them from the evil one.

*****

As a member of the Body of Christ we cannot live a Holy life when we allow things to be in our lives that the Holy Spirit is convicting us of. The more we read God's Word the cleaner we should become as the Word sanctifies us.

During ministry in the late 90's early 2000 we saw God deliver many Christians of demonic oppression, unfortunately they are not my testimonies to share. Needless to say, there were at least three ministers set free and one of those was in a public meeting at Driffield, North East Yorkshire, Uk. Unfortunately some well meaning ministers do not believe that Christians need any deliverance at all and so this gift is not widely used or accepted hence the people remain in a state of frustration not knowing what is wrong with them. Discern evil spirits and with God's wisdom, pray and deal with them. In the gospel of Mark chapter 16 Jesus speaks of signs and wonders that will follow believers and one of them is to cast out demons. God uses these gifts to reveal situations so that they can be dealt with, not for us to impress others.

As you can see from these gifts of Revelation they are usually in harmony with each other. Very rarely are they used on their own as wisdom is needed in them all. *"If any of you lacks wisdom, let him ASK GOD, that giveth to all men liberally, and upbraideth not; and it shall be given unto him."* James 1:5

Gifts of Inspiration

"There are different kinds of gifts but the same Spirit distributes them. There are different kinds of service, but the same Lord. There are different kinds of working, but in all of them and in everyone it is the same God at work. Now to each one the manifestation of the Spirit is given for the common good. To one there is given through the Spirit a message of wisdom, to another a message of knowledge by means of the same Spirit to another faith by the same Spirit, to another gifts of healing by that one

Spirit, to another miraculous powers, to another prophecy, to another distinguishing between spirits to another speaking in different kinds of tongues and to still another the interpretation of tongues. All these are the work of one and the same Spirit and he distributes them to each one, just as he determines." 1 Corinthians 12: 4–11 NIV

The gifts of Inspiration are:
- Prophecy
- Diverse Kinds of Tongues
- Interpretation of Tongues

Prophecy:
The gift of prophecy is not to be confused with the Office of a prophet we will cover this in a later chapter. Here Paul is speaking to the Corinthian Church *"But he who prophesies speaks edification and exhortation and comfort to men."* 1 Corinthians 14:4 We are to encourage one another with the word of God. If you receive a Word from God, write it down. In my own life as I read the Scriptures I sense a nudging from the Holy Spirit to send it to someone either by text, email or letter. It is usually a word that builds up, comforts and encourages and Paul exhorts us to have this gift more than any other.

The enemy, satan, is the author of confusion and even in the gifts of God he tries to manipulate, discredit and destroy the work of God. As we read many historical accounts in Scripture we can see him in operation even on what we consider the most Godly of men. David, as king of Israel committed adultery but eventually repented. Saul, Israel's first king was consumed with jealousy over David and tried to kill him a few times, to name a couple. When men prophecy and it does not come to pass God says they are False prophets. *"But the prophet who presumes to speak a word in My name, which I have not commanded him to speak, or who speaks in the name of other gods, that prophet shall die.*" Deuteronomy 18:20

In the Acts of apostles chapter 21 we can read of Agabus the prophet that bound Paul, "*And as we stayed many days, a certain prophet named Agabus came down from Judea. When he had come to us, he took Paul's belt, bound his own hands and feet, and said, 'Thus says the Holy Spirit, 'So shall the Jews at Jerusalem bind the man who owns this belt, and deliver him into the hands of the Gentiles.' Now when we heard these things, both we and those from that place pleaded with him not to go up to Jerusalem. Then Paul answered, 'What do you mean by weeping and breaking my heart? For I am ready not only to be bound, but also to die at Jerusalem for the name of the Lord Jesus.'*" We know of course that this prophecy came true.

All true prophecy is given by God through the power of the Holy Spirit. Counterfeits can prove disastrous for the sheep, it can steer them down the wrong path. We must begin to exercise these gifts and take them seriously. We should write them down and watch over them to see if they are from God or from men. Only by carefully monitoring these things will we begin to mature in the gifts.

Divers Kinds of Tongues:

"*Wherefore I give you to understand that no man speaking by the Spirit of God called Jesus accursed: and that no man can say that Jesus is Lord, but by the Holy Spirit.*" 1 Corinthians 12:3

It is imperative that we remember this Scripture concerning all the gifts we have mentioned as it is possible to manufacture counterfeits. One of the most controversial gifts, in my experience, is the gift of tongues. Mainly, I believe, as we do try to fit the Word of God to suit our own doctrine and to say what it is not saying.

"When the Day of Pentecost had fully come, they were all with one accord in one place. And suddenly there came a sound from heaven, as of a rushing mighty wind, and it filled the whole house where they were sitting. Then there appeared to them divided tongues, as of fire, and one sat upon each of them. And they were all filled with the Holy Spirit and began to speak with other tongues, as the Spirit gave them utterance."
Acts 2:1-4

The Crowd's Response

"And there were dwelling in Jerusalem Jews, devout men, from every nation under heaven. And when this sound occurred, the multitudes came together, and were confused because everyone heard them speak in his own language. Then they were all amazed and marvelled, saying to one another, 'Look, are not all those who speak Galileans? And how is it that we hear, each in our own language in which we were born? Parthians and Medes and Elamites, those dwelling in Mesopotamia, Judea and Cappadocia, Pontus and Asia, Phrygia and Pamphylia, Egypt and the parts of Libya adjoining Cyrene, visitors from Rome, both Jews and proselytes, Cretans and Arabs-we hear them speaking in our own tongues the wonderful works of God.' So they were all amazed and perplexed, saying to one another, 'Whatever could this mean?' Others mocking said, 'They are full of new wine.'" Acts 2:???

Hear we read of all these nations hearing of the wonderful works of God in their own tongue (the root word here is interpreted as dialect) as the Holy Spirit enabled them. This was amazing to everyone; it was what had been foretold by the prophet Joel. If we go back into the Old Testament we read of Jacob prophesying that God would take them back to the, *"Land of their Fathers"* Genesis 28:21. This is well before the Israelites lost their freedom and became captives in Egypt. This is just as amazing as seeing cloves of fire and listening to strangers speak in their native language about the wonders of God. Thousands bowed the knee that day and acknowledged Jesus as their Saviour. They gladly received His word and were baptised: and the same day around three thousand souls were added unto them.

Diverse kinds of tongues mean different kinds of tongues. Even though it is a Heavenly Language it can be spoken in many different ways as the Lord pleases. The speaking or interpretation of tongues can only be manifested by those who are baptised in the Holy Spirit for it is a spiritual language. I believe that is why there are so many arguments about this particular gift as you do have to be baptised in the Holy Spirit to know when it is God and when it is not.

"But God has revealed them to us through His Spirit. For the Spirit searches all things, yes the deep things of God. For what man knows the things of a man except the spirit of the man which is in him? Even so no one knows the things of God except the Spirit of God." 1 Corinthians 2:11

Paul, as he taught the Corinthian Church about the gifts of the Holy Spirit, says that different gifts are given to different people. He states *"...to another the working of miracles; to another prophecy; to another discerning of spirits; to another diverse kinds of tongues; to another the interpretation of tongues."* 1 Corinthians 12:10

Jesus Himself spoke to His disciples telling them of their future ministry in the Spirit and, of course, we must remember this is the resurrected Jesus speaking.

He told them to go into the entire world and preach the gospel to every creature. He said that those who believe and is baptised will be saved: but he that does not believe shall be damned. And these signs shall follow them that believe:

- In My name they shall cast out demons

- <u>They shall speak in new tongues</u>
- They shall take up serpents and if they drink any deadly thing it shall not harm them
- They shall lay hands on the sick and they will recover.

Mark chapter 16: 17-18

Here the interpretation of the word 'tongues' means language. Jesus says here they will speak in a new language. What language could that be? I believe a heavenly one. The word for tongues here has the same meaning as the one in 1 Corinthians 14: *"For he who speaks in a tongue does not speak to man but to God, for no one understands him; however, in the Spirit he speaks mysteries."*

Interpretation of Tongues:

It is wonderful to speak or sing to God in this language as our language seems insufficient to praise and worship Him. But can you imagine walking into a Church meeting and hearing everyone in their own tongues praising God and not a single word in your native tongue? You would not be able to understand or learn anything. It would be of little or no value to you. This is what Paul is explaining in, 1 Corinthians 14. Speaking in tongues will not win anyone for Christ if others cannot understand what is being said. However, if someone interprets what is being said in this heavenly language, they will be convicted of sin.

Its Correct Use

I run the risk here of putting God's precious gifts into a box in my effort to go deeper into explaining them. It is only as you read God's Word and experience the Holy Spirit for yourself will you begin to really understand. We should not departmentalise the wonderful person of the Holy Spirit for He is a person with all the attributes of God divinely imparted to us for the building up of the body of believers.

Because of the Corinthian Church's misuse of some of the gifts Paul tries to bring order among the believers for when they come together. Some argue that tongues only take the form of known languages spoken somewhere in the world. If speaking in tongues are only for interpretation of a native language then why do missionaries have to learn the language of the country they are sent to? When we have the gift of tongues we are able to sing in tongues, prophecy and interpret and in my own experience when I have given a tongue I Have known the person through whom the interpretation will come. I am not saying this is always the case for everyone but it has been for me.

In Conclusion

Acts 19: 5-7 states, *"...they spoke in tongues and prophesied after Paul laid hands upon them."* It also says in 1 Corinthians 14:5, *"I wish you all spoke with tongues, but even more that you prophesied; for he who prophesies is greater than he who speaks with tongues, unless indeed he interprets, that the church may receive edification."*

Let us try to understand this wonderful gift rather than throw it out of our theology because we do not understand it. If we do that we will not only miss out on the wonders of how God can use us but also a deeper intimacy with God through His Holy Spirit.

Further Scriptures to study are, 1 Corinthians 12, 13 & 14 as well as Acts 10. You can also find other books on these subjects that will go deeper than I have done here.

Chapter 10

Ministry Gifts of Christ

"It was He Jesus who gave some to be apostles, some to be prophets, some to be evangelists and some to be pastors and teachers. To prepare God's people for work of service so that the Body of Christ may be built up until we all reach the unity of the faith and in the knowledge of the Son of God and become mature attaining to the whole measure of the fullness of Christ." Ephesians 4:11-13 NIV (New International Version)

Up to now we have covered some of the gifts that are made manifest in a believer under the anointing of the Holy Spirit. We also know we have to be baptised in the Holy Spirit. He is the Baptiser and it is His Church. There are other gifts that are so important but these are given by Jesus Himself and they are different from those we just spoke about in the book of Corinthians.

In the Ephesians 4 passage above, we read of five offices of ministry gifts given by Jesus to His Body. They are:

- Teachers
- Pastors
- Evangelists
- Apostles

- Prophets

Why? For the EQUIPPING OF THE SAINTS:

It is so important that we understand these wonderful gifts Jesus has given and why. I believe one of the reasons that the body is not growing or experiencing any kind of revival is that these gifts are not acknowledged or nurtured in many of our churches.

These ministry gifts of Christ operate in the fullness of the Holy Spirit all the time, they are lifelong gifts and not like a nine to five job. It really is a call on someone's life, it never leaves you. If Jesus has put any of these gifts into you it is not for you to revel in but is for the building and equipping of the saints so that the body can grow. *"...and I say unto thee, that thou art Peter* (means stone) *and upon this rock* (original Greek, Petra) *I WILL BUILD MY CHURCH; and the gates of hell shall not prevail against it. I will give you the keys of the kingdom and whatever you bind on earth will be bound in heaven and whatever you loose on earth will be loosed in heaven."* Matthew 16:18

Jesus here, is in conversation with Peter, He is giving authority to Peter and stating He Himself (Jesus) is the rock on which He will build His Church. It was not built on Peter as his name means stone not rock. There is only one rock and that is Christ Jesus. It is very clear therefore, from the previous Scriptures that Jesus Himself will build His Church by giving certain gifts to men and women to equip the body so that it can be built up in the most Holy faith. We have already read that God has poured out His Spirit on all flesh, meaning His sons and His daughters, not the unsaved.

We are going to take each Ministry gift separately and break them down so they are easier to understand and give more insight as to how the Church is built. I pray it will also answer many questions as to why the Church itself needs to recognise the gifts.

These are not man appointed but God appointed gifts that operate under the anointing of the Holy Spirit with the authority of God Himself. These are not titles either these are offices, i.e. office of a pastor, office of a teacher, office of an apostle etc. This is not a hierarchy either, these gifts are of servanthood in nature and accountable to each other. In 1 Corinthians 4:1 it reads *"...let each man consider us as servants of Christ and stewards of the mysteries of God."*

It is sometimes difficult to recognise these gifts within yourself or others and that is why we need discernment and mature servants of the Lord to encourage and help us.

The Teacher:
"And He [Jesus] *gave some to be TEACHERS:"*

This is quite a straightforward ministry (office) as the clue is in the title. Yet, over the years, I have seen such misuse and lack of understanding of the gift of a teacher.

We have many men appointed teachers and I have witnessed believers put in charge of house groups to teach who do not even know their own Bible but yet are given a subject from their pastor to teach. The result is a boring group that leaves the group leader feeling they have failed. I have also seen where favouritism has been shown to certain people who were appointed to 'give a word' at the expense of the fellowship. What they end up sharing did not come from the Holy Spirit. That person was not called to teach so the body suffers yet again and so does that person. It causes more destruction than building up. This is like 'a square peg in a round hole.'

1 Timothy 1:7 reads, *"...desiring to be teachers of the law understanding neither what they say nor the things that affirm them."* There are people with gifts of teaching within the Church but not recognised or given an opportunity; so without the ministry of the teacher members stop attending and become frustrated because they are not being fed or enlightened by the Word of God, thus not fulfilled or maturing.

When you see or listen to a God appointed gift it is amazing how you can sit under that ministry and really enjoy being fed on God's Word. To be taught by a man or a woman of God who has been anointed by God is very enlightening. I had the privilege of being taught by a pastor/teacher. I could not wait to get to the meetings and did not want to leave. He could feed your spirit for days. The more he fed you, the more food you wanted and it encouraged me to want to search the Word for myself. He brought God's Word alive to me. I will be ever grateful to him and to God for him and I know I will meet him one day as he is in glory now.

Teachers will always be compelled to teach in every situation. Compelled by the Holy Spirit to teach the body. To teach is an awesome responsibility. It is the Holy Spirit who is ultimately the teacher that leads us into ALL TRUTH so the person who teaches must be led by the Holy Spirit and simply passing on what they received from Him.

In Hebrews 13:17 it states: *"Obey those who rule over you and be submissive for they watch out for your souls and must give an account, let them do so with joy and not grief which would be unprofitable for you."*

Nowadays there is much teaching around on DVD's, mobile apps, e-books, reading books, seminars, bible schools and courses on the internet. It is wonderful that we can access God's Word so freely but may I point out a word of caution? Please, please, please read your own

Bible before taking everything on board that you see and hear and be connected to others who you can be accountable to.

If you are a young Christian reading this and you are hungry to learn just like a baby needs milk, just remember to check everything against God's Word and *"...not be tossed around by every word of doctrine."* Ephesians 4: 14

This particular gift is not always in your fellowship/Church and as lovely as your pastor/elders might be, maybe they do not have the gift of teaching. This is where you need to feed yourself on the Word of God. Many teachers may have a specific subject that they have studied i.e. creation, end times, prayer, worship and many more. It comes from their heart and not from their head. It is good to invite a recognised teacher to your Church where you can interact, ask questions and really get into the subjects.

So, fairly straightforward. Just remember not everyone who teaches is necessarily a gifted teacher from Jesus to the Church. They may be trying their best under difficult situations. You can help them by reading for yourself as the best teacher is the Holy Spirit Himself. 1 John 24 -27

"Therefore let that abide in you which you heard from the beginning. If what you heard from the beginning abides in you, you also will abide in the Son and in the Father. And this is the promise that He has promised us-eternal life. These things I have written to you concerning those who try to deceive you. But the anointing which you have received from Him abides in you, and you do not need that anyone teach you; but as the same anointing teaches you concerning all things, and is true, and is not a lie, and just as it has taught you, you will abide in Him." 1 John 2:24-27

Always make sure that the Word of God has the last word and is not taken out of context. A text out of context leads to a pretext.[9] An example of this is in the gospel of John chapter 15 where Jesus says; *"You did not choose me, I chose you."* Today this is taken out of context to mean that God has chosen some people and no matter what they do or how they live, they will be saved. This passage is not saying that. If we take a closer look at the culture of the day you will understand that many groups of philosophers would stand at the gates of the city proclaiming their ideas. Those who gathered listened and, if they liked what the philosophers were saying and teaching, would become their followers. That's what Jesus meant. In this case however, we weren't the ones who chose Him but He selected/chose us to follow Him. In John 3:16 it says, *"God so loved the world that He gave his only Son that whosoever believes in Him shall have everlasting life."* So God loves the whole of mankind not just a few chosen ones.

When reading it is good to ask what is the situation and culture of the day? It is also good to use a concordance and maybe a history book to find out about the culture in the times of the Bible passage you are reading about. Many cults also take biblical text out of context to further their own doctrines. We can take a brief look at some of the New Testament teachers of the truth. Firstly teacher means instructor and the original Greek word is 'didaskalos.' (Young's Analytical Concordance)

In 1 John 3:2 it reads *"We know that thou art a teacher come from God."* This is of course speaking of Jesus Himself our ultimate teacher as in John chapter 1 it says *"In the beginning was the Word and the Word was with God and the Word was God."* and Verse 14 states *"...and the WORD became flesh and dwelt amongst us..."* Wow, so we know when

---

[9] Taking a Scripture out of its contextual meaning and making it mean something entirely different from what was intended by the writer.

we read our Bibles that we are reading about Jesus The Way, The Truth and The Life.

Paul in 2 Timothy 1:11 says: *"To which I was appointed a Preacher, an apostle and a teacher to the Gentiles."* In his first letter to Timothy Paul exhorts him to teach and instruct his fellowship. Timothy was a pupil of Paul's thus equipping him for the work of the ministry, proving here that Paul is an anointed man of God.

WARNING:

We need to understand that there are many false teachers amongst us. There was in Paul's day and even more in our day and generation, and it has accelerated as we approach the coming of our Lord Jesus. 2 Timothy 4:3 says *"For the time will come when they will not endure sound doctrine, but after their own lusts shall they heap to themselves teachers, having itching ears."* 2 Peter 2:1 states, *"But there were false prophets also among the people, even as there shall be false teachers among you, who privily shall bring in damnable heresies, even denying the Lord that bought them, and bring upon themselves swift destruction."*

Jesus said, *"These people draw near to Me with their mouth, and honor Me with their lips, but their heart is far from Me. and in vain they worship Me, teaching as doctrines the commandments of men."* Matthew 15:8-9

If we keep our heart in step with God's Word and seek the Holy Spirit as our teacher we will stay on that Narrow Path.

I exhort you to have a hungry heart for Jesus not itching ears running around to find something that suits you. The Word of God is alive and sharper than any two edged sword it changes us to be more like Jesus and to live in love, joy and peace in the Holy Spirit.

The Pastor:

Jesus gave some to be pastors for the equipping of the saints for the work of the ministry. The word pastor derives from the Latin noun pastor which means 'shepherd and relates to the Latin verb pascere – to lead to pasture, set to grazing, cause to eat.' (Wikipedia) https://en.wikipedia.org/wiki/Shepherd

So God called pastors to feed the sheep and not normal food either, but the Bread of the Word of God. Jesus said *"I am the living bread which came down from heaven. If anyone eats of this bread, he will live forever, and the bread that I shall give is My flesh, which I shall give for the life of the world."* John 6:51

A pastor is to meditate on the Word asking Jesus what to feed His people, after all they are Jesus' sheep and He will give them exactly what they need. He knows people's hearts and lives better than any man. I have experienced over and over again receiving that word from God that feeds the soul and nourishes and builds up. Jesus knows best!

If you were to ask most Christians today what the role of a pastor is they would probably say he visits people, preaches and runs a church, their own way. In many ways we have been conditioned into thinking these things by what we have seen and experienced. They may like to do these things but this is not the office/function of a pastor.

I have read a book called 'The Spirit of the Shepherd' by Meshach Paul Krikorian. Meshach was an Armenian shepherd boy, a survivor of atrocities, lover of all souls, lover of God, evangelist and preacher. He tells of his life tending, caring, guiding and protecting his sheep in the East on the border of Turkey and Iran. It is one of the most profound and wonderful, true life stories, of an actual Armenian Shepherd. This is an insight into a true Shepherd's heart for his sheep. After reading his account of shepherding sheep, I will never read Psalm 23 (The Shepherd's Psalm) the same again.

I love the way he knew every one of his sheep by name. How they would nibble his ear for attention, how they knew his voice and how he knew where to take them for good food and how to save them from the 'Valley of the Shadow' of death which is an actual valley. He describes its terrors and how he protected the sheep even to laying down his own life if needed. You sense his love for them and theirs for him. Jesus is even greater than this. He is 'The Good Shepherd' and you can read all about Him in John chapter 10.

I believe Meshachs Krikorian's book really puts into perspective the office of a pastor. I have known many good pastors who have given their all for the sheep and are still doing it. Why? They know that the sheep are Jesus' sheep, bought with a price, Jesus' precious blood.

I have also witnessed counterfeit men who thought they were a pastor but starved the sheep and are still doing so. In the book of Jeremiah there are many prophetic warnings for this kind of pastor.

"The shepherds are senseless and do not inquire of the LORD; so they do not prosper and all their flock is scattered." Jeremiah 10:21 This says it all I think.

"Woe to the shepherds who are destroying and scattering the sheep of my pasture!' declares the LORD. Therefore this is what the LORD, the God of Israel says to the shepherds who tend my people: 'Because you have scattered my flock and driven them away and have not bestowed care on them, I will bestow punishment on you for the evil you have done, declares the LORD. I will place shepherds over them who will tend them, and they will no longer be afraid or terrified, nor will any be missing,

declares the LORD." Jeremiah 23: 1- 4

Read the Prophecy of Ezekiel 34. This is a wonderful chapter from which I will take just a few extracts but please read this for yourself. It is a great promise from the Lord to the Nation of Israel and to us who belong to Jesus.

"The word of the LORD came to me 'Son of man, prophesy against the shepherds of Israel; prophesy and say to them: 'this is what the Sovereign LORD says: Woe to you shepherds of Israel who only take care of yourselves! Should not shepherds take care of the flock? You eat the curds, clothe yourselves with the wool and slaughter the choice animals, but you do not take care of the flock. You have not strengthened the weak or healed the sick or bound up the injured. You have not brought back the strays or searched for the lost. You have ruled them harshly and brutally. So they were scattered because there was no shepherd and when they were scattered they became food for all the wild animals. They were scattered over the whole earth, and no one searched or looked for them." (1-6)

"This is what the Sovereign LORD says: I am against the shepherds and will hold them accountable for my flock. I will remove them from tending the flock so that the shepherds can no longer feed themselves. I will rescue my flock from their mouths, and it will no longer be food for them." (7-9)

"I myself will tend my sheep and have them lie down, declares the Sovereign LORD. I will search for the lost and bring back the strays. I will bind up the injured and strengthen the weak, but the sleek and the strong I will destroy. I will shepherd the flock with justice." (15-16)

"I will place over them one shepherd, my servant David, and he will tend them; he will tend them and be their shepherd. I the LORD will be their God and my servant David will be prince among them." (23-24)

"You are my sheep, the sheep of my pasture, and I am your God, declares the Sovereign LORD." (31)

There are many warnings of the faithless shepherd throughout the Bible. This just makes us realise how God sees the seriousness of this office and how His warnings must be heeded as there will be consequences. The sheep or flock of God are of significant importance to Him, that He eventually sent The Great Shepherd to oversee them. His name is Jesus.

Jesus came to fulfil the law and the prophets and we see the fulfilment of this Ezekiel prophecy as He describes Himself in John chapter 10:14 *"I am the Good Shepherd. The Good Shepherd gives His life for the sheep..."* and as the Good Shepherd He states: *"I know MY sheep and MY sheep know ME."*

Any pastor called by God to shepherd the flock will get to know them and they will get to know the pastor, it is a ministry that requires deep and meaningful relationships.

The Evangelist:
God gave some to be an evangelist. Evangelist means one who announces Good news. Over the years I have attended many meetings when an evangelist came to town and always thought that an evangelist was someone who preached the gospel. I was once told by a pastor that an evangelist could, 'preach on mickey mouse and people would be saved.' What? As a young impressionable Christian I must say I found that extremely irreverent and a mockery of the atoning work of Jesus Christ. Obviously, over the years as I have studied God's Word I now know what he said was totally untrue and yes extremely irreverent.

It is the gospel of Jesus that saves souls and the work/office of an evangelist is to equip the Body of Christ for reaching unbelievers. They may preach the gospel but that is geared towards this objective and signs and wonders would follow the preaching to confirm the word to the hearer. Romans chapter 1 verse 16 Paul says: *"For I am not ashamed of the gospel of Christ for it is the power of God unto salvation to everyone who believes."*

An evangelist helps others to share their testimony. How they came to Jesus. He instructs them how to reach and communicate with the unbeliever. He encourages them to study the Word of God and have a deeper walk with Jesus. He shares knowledge of other cults etc... so they can discern truth from error and then be able to share that truth.

Above all, they need a baptism in the Holy Spirit because it is His work. We shared in earlier chapters that the Holy Spirit is The Teacher in all things pertaining to the Kingdom of God. This office of the evangelist usually works with other gifts i.e. pastor or teacher but most certainly an apostle. Most of these offices do not necessarily stand alone and you will find that if you actually study Church History usually God gives two or three or maybe all of the gifts to be used in the power and anointing of the Holy Spirit. This is all for the direct purpose of equipping the Body to extend God's Kingdom and ultimately bring God glory.

Let us take a look at Peter's ministry:

In Acts chapter 2 he received knowledge from God on what was happening when the Holy Spirit fell. He identified the Holy Spirit. With great power he told everyone this had been foretold. He began to preach about Jesus, His death and resurrection. Under the anointing people were cut to the heart and asked what they could do to be saved. Peter did not mince his words, *"Repent of your sins and be baptised everyone of you and you shall receive the gift of the Holy Spirit."* Over

3000 souls repented and were baptised in one day.

When you study Peter's ministry you can see how many offices he held and what gifts he moved in. Nothing seemed withheld from him as he gave his life over to God. Yes, you are right, this was the frightened Peter who denied Jesus three times the night He was arrested.

One of the obvious traits of an evangelist is prayer. They are always praying for souls and the Body of Christ. Prayer has legs so don't be surprised when you pray for someone that you are also given the opportunity to talk of Jesus to them.

Evangelism is not just witnessing, it is to make it clear to the unbeliever that they have sinned against God and will stand before Him to give an account. That there is a punishment for sin and yes it is called hell and it is a place of torment. Not merely separation from God.

"And in Hell he lifted up his eyes, being in torment and sees Abraham afar off and Lazarus in his bosom. He cried and said Father Abraham have mercy on me and send Lazarus that he may dip the tip of his finger in water and cool my tongue for I am tormented in this flame." Luke 16:23-24

Evangelism is the believer assuring the unbeliever of which Jesus he is talking about. (See 2 Corinthians 11:4) It is the believer convincingly portraying Jesus as fully man and fully God yet without sin.

Nothing has changed. The way to God is still the same for us all. Repentance for sin and accepting that Jesus is the Son of the Living God, who paid the price for our sins with His own precious blood. These are just a few examples of witnessing and I pray they will be of help to you. This subject could be a book on its own. But it is all under the leading, guiding and empowering of the Holy Spirit.

Most of the apostles and disciples stayed together to help and teach each other the things they had learned from Jesus. They were also accountable to each other until eventually they were scattered due to persecution.

The Prophet:

"The ordinary Hebrew word for prophet is nabi, derived from a verb signifying 'to bubble forth' like a fountain; hence the word means one who announces or pours forth the declarations of God. The English word comes from the Greek 'prophetes' (pro-fe-tes), which signifies in classical Greek one who speaks for another, especially one who speaks for a god." Smith's Bible dictionary.

Again this is an important office and means someone who hears directly from God and delivers the message to God's people. Its objective is to bring direction and correction. The prophet will usually bring the Word of God and his heart's desire is to see the Body of Christ grow in obedience and love towards God. An example in the old testament is Samuel. There had been no word or direction in Israel for over 400 years so God raised up Samuel. The people began to see that Samuel was no ordinary man, he was a man of God. God showed him Israel's first and second king and he brought the word of God back to Israel. There are numerous examples in the Old Testament of the office of a prophet. Part of his job was to anoint kings publicly and to steer people away from rebellion against God.

Today we have the Word of God, Jesus, and He speaks to us through men of the word bringing direction for our lives. *"In former days God has spoken to us by His prophets but in these last days He has spoken to us through His Son."* Hebrews chapter 1, and in Matthew 5:17 Jesus says: *"Think not that I came to destroy the law, or the prophets. I am not come to destroy but to fulfil."* This is a call and an office that needs much clarification as again it is so needed in the Body of Christ in our nation and the nations of the world.

In the Old Testament in Zechariah 7:12 it says: *"Yea, they made their hearts as an adamant stone, lest they should hear the law, and the words which the Lord of Hosts has sent in His Spirit by the former prophets: therefore came a great wrath from the Lord of Hosts."*

Jesus said in Matthew 23:27 *"O Jerusalem, Jerusalem, the one who kills the prophets and stones those who are sent to her! How often I wanted to gather your children together, as a hen gathers her chicks under her wings, but you were not willing."*

Most of the prophets message to Israel was to repent and turn from their wicked ways. Unfortunately we do not want to hear that sort of message from the prophets of today, we would rather listen to a popular speaker who tickles our ears and make us feel good.

The office of a prophet is to guide and help God's people to stay on the narrow path. This is not done through his own words, opinion or any kind of psychological training. Prophecy is the speaking forth of God's Word empowered by the Holy Spirit. These words brings solutions, a moving forward and above all a closer relationship with the Lord. Therefore, it is essential that a prophet know and study God's Word and have that deep relationship with Jesus Christ as they move in the power of the Holy Spirit.

This office, along with the apostle, is also one of the foundations upon which Jesus builds His Church.

Jesus speaking in Matthew 7 says: *"Enter through the narrow gate for wide is the gate and broad is the road that leads to destruction, and many enter through it, but small is the gate and narrow the road that leads to life, and only a few find it."*

When you are in God's Word continually because you have a sincere desire to fulfil His Kingdom's purposes, you will find that you can become a more effective prophet as the word changes you to become more like Christ, who was the greatest of all prophets. It is God's Word that has the power, not man's, and when spoken under the anointing of the Holy Spirit will bring about amazing results for those who respond to it.

I have been in the position where God gives me a word of prophecy and it was quite frightening to have to give something other than the usual expected nice little message. It takes a lot of faith to believe that God wants you to speak out what He has told you.

I was invited to speak at a local church and God impressed upon me to preach on Sodom and Gomorrah and the consequences of living in sin. To tell them that Ichabod (meaning the glory of the Lord has departed) was written over the portals of the door and that He is calling the church to repent. I knew of nothing that was going on in the fellowship at that time or anything of the people that worshipped there. I remember feeling very nervous and concerned that I would upset people and yet I knew the message was right. It was very uncomfortable for me but important to give out what God had given me.

The Church in question did not heed that warning and it ended up not only closing but being torn down. Apart from the church itself suffering, the people in that area had no real witness of Jesus. I ask you this question; did God receive any Glory from their disobedience?

No, but what could have happened if by a step of faith someone in that church received the word, acted upon it and brought repentance? Possibly revival and renewal.

As you can see if one is to be a prophet and do this regularly they must be called by God. We have the wonderful assurance of Scripture that says when God calls He equips you; so that in turn we can help others to develop and help them in their ministry.

"For prophecy never came by the will of man, but Holy men of God spoke as they were moved by the Holy Spirit." 2 Peter: 1:21

In the Old Testament the prophets would seem to band together in groups. *"After that you shall come to the hill of God where the Philistine garrison is. And it will happen, when you have come there to the city, that you will meet a group of prophets coming down from the high place with a stringed instrument, a tambourine, a flute, and a harp before them; and they will be prophesying."* 1 Samuel 10:5. There are more similar Scriptures in Samuel and in Kings (see chapter 22).

If you are looking to be liked and accepted take heed of Jesus words in John 4:44 *"Now Jesus Himself had pointed out that a prophet has no honor in his own country."* Let us take a look at some of the Old Testament prophets and see how they were treated. Fifty five in all and let us remember they were men and women not robots.

1 Kings from chapter 18:1-4 is an account of the brutality of Jezebel, king Ahab's wife, to the prophets of God. She wanted them all dead and to put her own false prophets in their place. Fortunately Obadiah who was in charge of Ahab's house feared the Lord greatly and so took a hundred of God's prophets and hid them in caves, protected them and fed them even during a famine in the land. Although there was final

victory for Elijah he went through fear and near death just because he was a prophet.

There are many accounts of how the prophets in the Old Testament suffered. Here are examples of their suffering and afflictions...

"Nearly all of the prophets had a pretty rough time. Jeremiah, because of the Word he brought from the Lord, finds himself in a pit in prison, sinking deep into the mire (Jeremiah. 37 and 38). Tradition says Isaiah was sawn asunder. Daniel was put into the den of lions. Elijah was forced to flee from wicked queen Jezebel. Micaiah refused to tell anything but the Word of the Lord, even though he knew it would greatly displease Ahab. He was put in prison and fed on the bread of affliction. Joseph was a prophet, too, who suffered greatly. First he was sold into Egypt, then falsely accused and imprisoned there. The things they suffered were numerous: Some of them are listed in Hebrews 11:36-38: *'And others had trial of cruel mockings and scourgings, yea, moreover of bonds and imprisonment: they were stoned, they were sawn asunder, were tempted, were slain with the sword: they wandered about in sheepskins and goatskins; being destitute, afflicted, tormented; of whom the world was not worthy.'"* [10]

Isaiah chapter 9, foretold the coming of the Messiah (Jesus). Most of the messages would begin calling Israel to repent. The message for the church and the world is no different today, but the consequences of sin and the need for repentance seem to be left out of most prophetic preaching. Some of the last words Jesus spoke in the book of Revelation are "Repent" or else. In the first 3 chapters of Revelations He also says; *"...he that hath an ear let him hear what the Spirit says to the churches."*

At the beginning we opened with Hebrews chapter 1 *"In former days*

---

[10] https://www.studyjesus.com/Religion_Library/James/47_Patience-Prophets.htm

God spoke to us by his prophets BUT IN THESE LAST DAYS HE HAS SPOKEN TO US THROUGH HIS SON...JESUS." THE PROPHET, PRIEST AND SOON COMING KING. Jesus speaks to us through His Word. Jesus always has the last say.

Warning of False Prophets:

Let us begin by just looking at a few Scriptures where we are told to 'beware' of False prophets:-

- *"Watch out for false prophets they come to you in sheep's clothing, but inwardly they are ferocious wolves."* Matthew 7:15
- *"Beloved, do not believe every spirit, but test the spirits, whether they are of God; because many false prophets have gone out into the world."* 1 John 4:1
- *"For false christs and false prophets will rise and show signs and wonders to deceive, if possible, even the elect."* Mark 13:22

Jesus speaks prophetically in Matthew 24, about the signs of the times at the end of the world and when we read that chapter it can be quite alarming. He gave us the warnings above because we can be deceived; so we need to be on our guard against false prophets. Therefore, whenever you hear a prophetic word remember if it is not in line with God's Word and in the correct interpretation then question it, ask the Holy Spirit and another Holy Spirit filled person to confirm or negate what you have heard.

There is much more to being a prophet of the Lord than I have written here but I pray you have a closer insight into the office of a prophet and will not easily be led astray by false prophets and doctrines of men.

The Apostle:

"The term 'apostle' is derived from Classical Greek (ἀπόστολος apóstolos), meaning 'one who is sent away', from (στέλλω 'stello', 'send') + (από apo, 'away from'). The word 'apostle' has two meanings, the broader meaning of a messenger and the narrow meaning of an early Christian apostle directly linked to Jesus." Wikipedia

"And He gave some to be apostles for the equipping of the saints for the work of the ministry for the edifying of the Body of Christ." Ephesians 4:11-12

*"Now, therefore, you are no longer strangers and foreigners, but fellow citizens with the saints and members of the household of God having been built on the foundation of the apostles and prophets, Jesus Christ Himself being the Chief Cornerstone, in whom the whole building, being fitted together, grows into a holy temple in the Lord, in whom you also are being built together for a dwelling place of God in the Spirit."*Ephesians 2:28

Here Paul is explaining to the Ephesians Church how the offices of the apostle and the prophet are the foundation on which the Church is built with Jesus Christ Himself being the Chief Cornerstone. The meaning of apostle as derived from Scriptures is 'one sent forth' and is full of the Holy Spirit; equipped by Jesus to begin a new work. He cooperates with the Holy Spirit, having a mandate from God as to where to go and begin telling the good news of Jesus Christ with the message of sin, repentance and salvation through the blood of Jesus. If there is no blood mentioned or what Jesus accomplished on the cross, the consequences of sin, or the need for repentance in their message then may I dare suggest, it is not the message the true gospel of Jesus Christ? It is possible that such a person is not an anointed apostle of Christ.

Paul was sent to Macedonia, Troas Philippi, Asia, Rome and Jerusalem. As you read his amazing exploits in the book of Acts you will see how many churches he started all in the power of the Holy Spirit. *"And I, brethren, when I came to you, I did not come with excellence of speech or of wisdom declaring to you the testimony of God. For I determined not to know anything among you except Jesus Christ and Him crucified. I was with you in weakness, in fear, and in much trembling. And my speech and my preaching were not with persuasive words of human wisdom, but in demonstration of the Spirit and of power that your faith should not be in the wisdom of men but in the power of God."* 1 Corinthians 2:1-5

I always wondered why this strong bold apostle said that he was in weakness, fear and trembling. This Paul who had tasted more lashes of the whip and imprisonment for the gospel than any other. Who was not afraid to challenge the Jewish leaders and tell them they no longer needed the law. I believe his fear and trembling was because he wanted only what the Holy Spirit wanted. It was not fear of the Church but the ultimate reverent fear of God. We need more of this kind of reverence in our day and generation. I believe Paul was terrified of not being 'in the Spirit', how much more should we?

In today's society we have learned marketing techniques, selling, how to go door to door with designed programmes to begin a work of God. Friends, it is the Power of the Holy Spirit we need, working through us modern day Spirit filled believers with a message from God and sent by God. True apostles.

We also know that Paul performed many miracles under the anointing of the Holy Spirit. So an apostle is equipped for every good work that God has anointed and appointed him to do. Paul also said: *"I became all things to all men that I might win some, to the weak I became as weak, that I might gain the weak: I am all things to all men that I might by all means save some."* 1 Corinthians 9:22 Here Paul is also evangelizing, giving some instruction on how to save souls. We even quote this today over 2000 years later when we are trying to win souls for Jesus. This confirms what I said earlier that these three ministry gifts tend to work together.

All are to bring glory to God for the extension of His Kingdom.

I love Paul's letter to Timothy. *"I thank Christ Jesus our Lord who has given me strength, that He considered me faithful, appointing me to His service even though I was once a blasphemer and a persecutor and a violent man. I was shown mercy because I acted in ignorance and unbelief."* NIV (New International Version) 1 Timothy 1:12-15

What a wonderful man Paul turned out to be when he surrendered to the call of God. How he taught the Church so much by his own example. What an amazing apostle and even though there were and are apostles today Paul stands out as the chief amongst them. May I at this point encourage you to study his life and the great exploits he did for God; through the gifts and power of the Holy Spirit working in his life.

Chapter 11

Things that Grieve the Holy Spirit

"...and grieve not the Holy Spirit of God, whereby ye are sealed unto the day of redemption." Ephesians 4:30. The Holy Spirit is a person and a gentleman He can be grieved just like we can, only He is focused on the Kingdom of God and bringing glory to God. He also, being a gentleman, will never force His way into our lives. To prevent us from grieving Him we need to understand the things that do so we can avoid them. Just like in any relationship when we grow closer to another person, say in a marriage, we learn what our spouse likes and dislikes and through love we try very hard not to do or say anything to cause upset.

Some of the things that grieve Him are:

Unbelief

In Matthew 13:58 Jesus could not do many miracles in His own town because of their lack of belief. Similarly, today the Holy Spirit will not work miracles where there is unbelief.

Criticism

In 2 Samuel chapter 6 Michal, Saul's daughter despised David for dancing before the Ark of the Covenant and the result of that was barrenness.

Jealousy

In 1 Samuel 31 Saul was consumed with jealousy over David's popularity and success. He became possessed by evil spirits and eventually ended his own life by falling on his sword.

Disunity

In Numbers 12 Miriam was struck with leprosy because she murmured about her brother Moses taking a Midianite wife who was not of the same religion. Whatever the issue she should not have murmured against her brother. Just like us today we should not murmur against our brethren. (I call her murmuring Miriam)

Hard hearts

In Ephesians 4:30, Acts 7:51, Hebrews 3:7-8 we see people resisting the Holy Spirit. In Matthew 19:8 Jesus told the multitude that had gathered, that Moses had allowed divorce because of the hardness of their hearts. Isaiah 63:10 says; *"But they rebelled and grieved His Holy Spirit;"* Rebellion against the Holy Spirit grieves Him as does rebellion against God.

There are many accounts of these, our human failings but as Paul has said, *"If we follow after the Spirit we will not fulfil the lusts of the flesh."*

In Galatians 5:16 it says, *"So I SAY, LIVE BY THE SPIRIT and you will not gratify the desires of the sinful nature. For the desires of the sinful nature desires what is contrary to the Spirit and the Spirit what is contrary to the sinful nature. They are in conflict with one another so that you do not do what you want. But if you are led by the Spirit you are not under the law. For the acts of the sinful nature are obvious.*

- *Sexual immorality*
- *Impurity and debauchery*
- *Idolatry and witchcraft*
- *Hatred*

- *Discord and Jealousy*
- *Fits of rage*
- *Selfish ambition*
- *Dissensions and factions*
- *Envy*
- *Drunkenness*
- *Orgies and the like*

I warn you as I did before that those who live like this will not inherit the Kingdom of God."

"But the fruit of the Spirit is:

- *Love*
- *Joy*
- *Peace*
- *Patience*
- *Kindness*
- *Goodness*
- *Faithfulness*
- *Gentleness*
- *Self-control*

Against such things there is no law. Those who belong to Jesus Christ have crucified the sinful nature with its passion and desires. Since we live by the Spirit let us keep in step with the Spirit. Let us not become conceited, provoking each other and envying each other." The fruit of the Spirit is real evidence of a Holy Spirit filled person.

Paul puts it so well when he says to the Galatians Church, *"You foolish Galatians who has bewitched you that you should not obey the truth, before whose eyes Jesus Christ hath been evidently set forth, crucified among you? Are you so foolish having begun well in the Spirit…who cut in on you? How is it you now do things in the flesh?"* Galatians chapter 3

As I said at the beginning we can try things in our own strength and account it to the Holy Spirit and here Paul lets us know it was happening in his day too. We do need to learn that we can end up doing things in our own strength and it does not bring glory to God it just strokes our own ego. May God forgive us!

Blasphemy of the Holy Spirit:

There has been so much misconception of this passage in Matthew 12:31-32 that it deserves more than a mention; *"Wherefore I say unto you all manner of sin and blasphemy will be forgiven but blasphemy against the Holy Ghost shall not be forgiven unto men. And whosoever speaketh a word against the son of Man it shall be forgiven him: but whosoever speaketh against the Holy Spirit it shall not be forgiven him, neither in this world or the world to come."* These are the words of Jesus so we should take them absolutely seriously and take time to understand what He is saying. After all there is NO forgiveness for blasphemy of the Holy Spirit.

Over the years I have heard many explanations of this but one night the truth was revealed to me as I studied this passage of Scripture. Let us look at who was speaking and to whom He was speaking, and in what context?

Jesus has just been accused, by the religious leaders, of casting out a demon by the spirit of Beelzebub. Jesus' reply was, *"...a house divided against itself cannot stand."* They had credited a work of God to satan by accusing Jesus. So it is quite simple, blasphemy is giving satan the glory for what God has done. We can blaspheme the Holy Spirit, not when we take the Lord's name in vain, but when we give glory to satan for something God has done.

We serve such a Holy, loving and forgiving God so it is difficult to understand why this particular sin of the blasphemy of the Holy Spirit is unforgivable. Personally I think it is very difficult for a Christian to do. But we do need to know about it and take heed.

Chapter 12

Do I have the Holy Spirit?

The question now is, "Do I have the Holy Spirit?" but let's first look at receiving Him.

How do we receive Him?
This is a question I am often asked and the answer is very simple, faith. You need only believe.

John the Baptist said to the people who came out to be baptised by him, *"I baptise you with water but one more powerful than I will baptise you with the Holy Spirit and with Fire."* Luke 3:16 This is a prophetic word from John who is proclaiming that Jesus is the one to come after him. We see Jesus echoing John's words saying, *"John baptised with water but in a few days from now you will receive the Holy Spirit, wait in Jerusalem,"* and of course the outpouring happened, see Acts 2.

Jesus explains the benefit of His departure in John 16, *"But now I go away to Him who sent me and none of you asks me, where are you going? But because I have said these things to you, sorrow has filled your heart. Nevertheless, I tell you the truth. It is to your advantage that I go away, for if I do not go away, the helper will not come to you, but if I depart, I will send Him to you."* This is still happening to those who want more of God today in the 21st century.

The crowd to whom Peter spoke in Jerusalem after the Holy Spirit was poured out were greatly affected by what they had seen and heard. I believe they were convicted of their sin against God. They asked him; *"...what shall we do?"* Peter answered them and said; *"...repent and let everyone of you be baptised in the name of Jesus Christ for the remission of sin and you shall receive the gift of the Holy Spirit."*

The Holy Spirit is a gift from God to all those who believe in the Lord Jesus Christ and are baptised. All we have to do is accept that gift. Remember the example of the light switch? Just because we can't see the power does not mean it is not there. You can stop reading right now if you want to and pray for the gift. It is just a simple prayer and if said in the sincerity of your heart the Lord will answer you. He is more willing to give than we are to receive.

A short prayer

"Our Father, who art in heaven I repent of any unconfessed sin. I desire more of You and Your Holy Spirit in my life to live the life You intended for me. Help me in my daily walk with You and for the work in Your Kingdom. I give myself unreservedly to You. Please baptise me today and fill me to overflowing with Your Spirit. Feed me Your Word. Please hear and answer my heart's cry that You may be glorified in my life. In anticipation, I thank You with all my heart, Amen."

How will I know if I have received the Holy Spirit?

You will notice a change in your attitude and your speech. If you used to use bad language that will cease and you will begin to feel convicted if you do swear. You will feel offended if you are in company of people who take the Lord's name in vain. You will be hungry for God's Word as He is the teacher He will want you to know the rule book. You will want to be with others who are Spirit filled. You will want to speak to God all the time it, is called prayer. Don't worry how to do it just talk with God. You may even begin to speak in a peculiar/unknown language and this is called speaking with new tongues. Most of all you will want to tell others of Jesus and of your new found love and freedom in Christ. Your body has now become a temple for the Holy Spirit as written in Scriptures.

At this point I would like to quote from a book by Dr R A Torrey; entitled 'Why God used D L Moody'. He had this to say:

"The seventh thing that was the secret why God used D L Moody was that he had a very definite enduement with power from on high, a very clear and definite baptism with the Holy Ghost: He had no doubt about it. In his early days he was a great hustler: he had tremendous desire to do something but he had no real power. He worked very largely in the energy of the flesh. But there were two humble Free Methodist women who used to come over to his meetings in the YMCA. One was Aunty Cook and the other was Mr.s Snow. These two women would come to Mr Moody at the close of his meetings and say, 'We are praying for you'. Finally Mr Moody became somewhat nettled and said to them one night: 'Why are you praying for me? Why don't you pray for the unsaved?' They replied, 'We are praying that you may get the power'. Mr Moody did not know what they meant, but he got to thinking about it, and then went to these women and said: 'I wish you would tell me what you mean' and they told him about the definite baptism in the Holy ghost. Then he asked if he might pray with them and not merely have them pray for him.

Aunty Cook once told me of the intense fervour with which Mr Moody prayed on that occasion. She told me in words that I scarcely dare repeat, though I have never forgotten them. He not only prayed with them but he also prayed alone.

Not long after, one day on his way to England, he was walking up Wall Street in New York (Mr Moody very seldom told this and I almost hesitate to tell it) and in the midst of the hustle and bustle of that city his prayer was answered: The power of God fell upon him as he walked up the street and he had to hurry off to the house of a friend and ask that he might have a room for himself, and in that room he stayed alone for hours: and the Holy Ghost came upon him, filling his soul with such joy that at last he had to ask God to withhold His Hand, lest he die on the very spot with joy. He went from that place with the power of the Holy Ghost upon him and when he got to London England the power of God wrought through him mightily in North London and hundreds were added to the Church and that was what led to his being invited over for the wonderful campaign that followed in later years."[11]

What an amazing testimony of someone's desire for more of God, Oh that we would seek this power that would save hundreds of souls that are perishing without God.

"What? Know that your body is a temple of the Holy Spirit which is in you, which you have of God and you are not your own? For you were bought with a price therefore glorify God in your body and in your spirit which are God's." 1 Corinthians 6:19-20

[11] https://www.wholesomewords.org/biography/biomoody6.html

Chapter 13

The World Cannot Receive Him

Not anyone can see or receive the Holy Spirit He is sent to those who belong to Jesus Christ. I have heard many people speak of the Holy Spirit and yet it is obvious from their lifestyle, speech and lack of moral values that they do not know Him. Those who belong to Jesus can know the Holy Spirit as a personal friend and that is tremendous news. He has not left us as orphans, we need never feel alone again.

Jesus Promises: *"If you love Me, keep My commandments. And I will pray the Father, and He will give you another Helper, that He may abide with you forever— the Spirit of truth, whom the world cannot receive, because it neither sees Him nor knows Him; but you know Him, for He dwells with you and will be in you. I will not leave you orphans; I will come to you."* John 14:15-18 NKJV

There are different cults that suggest they are serving God but there is no Holy Spirit within them neither repentance from sin or salvation in Jesus Christ. There are also many other spirits which are not of the Kingdom of God and these wage war against the Holy Spirit too. This of course is another subject for another time.

I pray that the Holy Spirit is more real to you now and that you can see HIM as a person and not some sort of ghostly apparition or force. That without Him we have no power in building the Kingdom of God as we need His anointing (unction) to function. Sometimes we are led by Him into the unknown, but we trust in God for the final results and give Him ALL the glory.

You Must First be 'Born Again'

In John's gospel Chapter 3 there is a well known story of Nicodemus who was a religious leader, a Pharisee[12] and a member of the Sanhedrin. He had obviously been watching Jesus and listening to some of the miraculous stories about people who had met with Him. Nicodemus was no fool and he obviously had a good reputation amongst the religious leaders so he asked to see Him alone secretly during the night. He wanted to ask Jesus some very serious questions, after all, possibly everything he had ever known and learned was being challenged by the things Jesus said and did.

As a Pharisee, he did believe in the resurrection from the dead so he asked Him what he should do to enter the Kingdom of Heaven and Jesus replied, *"...you must be born again."* This must have startled Nicodemus as he thought he already had a pass into heaven through the law, but Jesus did not discuss those things with him. He just said, *"YOU MUST BE born again."* After that statement Jesus goes on to explain that this is a spiritual experiences not head knowledge, a law or political movement.

This was very difficult for Nicodemus to take in and just like today it is difficult for people to take it in or understand. But at the very least he

---

[12] The Pharisees were at various times a political party, a social movement, and a school of thought in the Holy Land during the time of the Second Temple Judaism. (Wikipedia)

wanted to search out the truth. Some want to earn salvation with good works or by belonging to some sect that believes they have the truth. The Watchtower Bible and Tract Society believe they are the only way to God. Nicodemus could not understand it and many today cannot understand it because it is a spiritual experience that begins with you believing the gospel.

I will never forget the night I surrendered my life to Jesus. He instantly became real to me even though I did not understand the full implication of what I had done or why I had to do it. It was in Radcliffe Tabernacle Lancashire and I had been invited by a relative. As a child I had been in the local church choir in my hometown of Chesterton, Newcastle-Under-Lyme in the Church of England but I had never heard the gospel of Jesus Christ like this before. It was such a warm, happy and vibrant church and everyone seemed so full of joy. They sang about Jesus like they knew Him and the preacher, Jim Sweet, even cried when he talked about Jesus on the cross. This was all new to me. Even though I knew nothing of the Bible I just knew everything he was saying about Jesus was true… there was an inner witness that I later realised was the Holy Spirit witnessing to my spirit. I was enthralled but it was when Jim finally said, "Jesus put two arms up for you, can't you put one up for Him?"

Well my arm shot in the air as if I had been pierced through and I was born again the very same second. That was my first encounter with Jesus… fantastic and I just knew, that I knew, that something special had happened to me inside my heart and spirit. I also had an immediate assurance that I was heaven bound. All my past seemed to rush in front of me and I started to cry as I realised God's love had reached out to even me. I was thirty two years old. This must be the greatest mysterious miracle that happens to all who will believe on the Lord Jesus Christ and His atoning work upon the cross.

From that day forth up to now, over 40 years I can honestly say with the apostle Paul: *"For I am not ashamed of the gospel of Christ, for it is the power of God to salvation for everyone who believes, for the Jew first and also for the Greek."* Romans 1:16

There are many sincere believers that are not born again so, can I ask you? Where do you stand? Being born again is a regeneration of your spirit by the Holy Spirit, it is His work. It is not a head decision or based on works where we strive to be good by giving to charity etc. (although all these are good). No, we can get into the Kingdom of Heaven only by being born again. Jesus' words not mine.

Keith Green (famous Christian songwriter) wrote a wonderful song about the Sheep and the Goats which is the story Jesus told in the book of Matthew. Some of the words are very humorous but carry much truth. He wanted to get the message across that going to Church does not make you a Christian just like going to Mcdonalds does not make you a Hamburger. A day is coming when Jesus will return (John chapter 14) and He will separate the real sheep from the goats. This means He will separate those who belong to Him from those who do not.

Make that sincere decision today to recognise Jesus as the Son of the Living God and accept Him as your Saviour. He will forgive you and cleanse you from sin. He will baptise you in the wonderful Holy Spirit and all you need to do is have faith and only believe, yes, only believe. Hope and love will enter your heart and life and all things will become new to you.

JESUS IS ALIVE. I know this from personal experience. He is more real to me everyday and has never left me in over 40 years. I was baptized in the Holy Spirit all those years ago and still desire more of Him. I have seen Jesus heal, baptize and set people free from demons all through the power of the Holy Spirit, who was poured out at Pentecost and is still here to fill hungry hearts.

Jesus is still baptizing believers in the Holy Spirit today, that is, those who will trust Him.

May I ask you? Have you been born again? Have you had this wonderful baptism in the Holy Spirit? If not, you only need to ask Jesus sincerely.

The Holy Spirit is not a force or ghostly apparition. He is a person. The work of our regeneration is by the power of the Holy Spirit and we have to realize that no one can enter the Kingdom unless he is first born again. Jesus has kept His promise to us. Let us eagerly desire to walk in the Spirit and not in the flesh so we can serve Jesus in His kingdom being co-workers together with Him and being filled with the Holy Spirit.

"Most assuredly I say to you he who believes in Me, the works that I do he will do also: and greater works than these he will do because I go to My Father. And whatever you ask in My name, that I will do, that the Father may be glorified in the Son. If you ask anything in MY NAME I WILL DO IT." John 14:12-14

We are a supernatural people and my prayer is that you have found this book helpful in your walk with Jesus and that you seek the Holy Spirit to enable you to truly function within the Body of Christ.

It is time for us all to say, "SIT DOWN FLESH MAN, RISE UP SPIRIT MAN!"

A Further Acknowledgement

This small contribution to the work of the Holy Spirit would not be complete without a prophetic Word given by a great apostle of Faith, now in Glory. He died in 1947, the year I was born.

As a new Christian I was thrilled at His work in the Kingdom of God and he greatly influenced my life in seeking the Holy Spirit. He is non other than Smith Wigglesworth.

Smith Wigglesworth's Prophecy;

"During the next few decades there will be two distinct moves of the Holy Spirit across the Church in Great Britain. The first move will affect every church that is open to receive it, and will be characterised by a restoration of the baptism and gifts of the Holy Spirit. The second move of the Holy Spirit will result in people leaving historic churches and planting new churches.

In the duration of each of these moves, the people who are involved will say, 'This is a great revival.' But the Lord says, 'No, neither is this the great revival but both are steps towards it.'

When the new Church phase is on the wane, there will be evidence in the churches of something that has not been seen before: a coming together of those with an emphasis on the Word and those with an emphasis on the Spirit. When the Word and the Spirit come together, there will be the biggest move of the Holy Spirit that the nation and indeed, the world has ever seen. It will mark the beginning of a revival that will eclipse anything that has been witnessed within these shores, even the Wesleyan and Welsh revivals of former years.

The outpouring of God's Spirit will flow over from the United

Kingdom to mainland Europe, and from there, will begin a missionary move to the ends of the earth."[13]

[13] The Way of the Spirit http://www.thewayofthespirit.com/smith-wigglesworths-prophecy/

About the Author

Barbara has been passionate for Jesus since her encounter with Him over 40 years ago and was immediately drawn into the Holy Bible where she found that the truth really does set you free from anxieties and sickness. She has taken God at His word in His healing power where she has been healed of many illnesses including epilepsy.

For over 30 years she has set up and led intercessory prayer groups, women's ministry, led in worship, ministered the gospel in song. She also preaches the gospel as well as teaching discipleship whilst also co-pastured a church in Rochdale. At present she lives in Grimsby with her husband John she has two sons and 4 grandchildren. Barbara is still leading people to Christ and preaching the gospel as He alone is the only answer to Life.

In a synopsis, she is an intercessor, worship leader, Bible teacher and minister.

Contact Me

I would love to hear your testimony after reading this book:-

Email me
paynebarbara7@gmail.com

Made in the USA
Monee, IL
07 July 2026

56544397R00075